THE KUNG OF THE KALAHARI

THE Kung OF THE Kalahari

BY
WALTER L. BATEMAN

Illustrated by
Richard C. Bartlett

UNITARIAN UNIVERSALIST
ASSOCIATION

Boston

Library of Congress catalog card number: 72-121824
International Standard Book Number: 0-8070-1898-8
The Unitarian Universalist Association, Boston 02108
Text Copyright © 1970 by Walter L. Bateman
Illustrations Copyright © 1970 by Richard C. Bartlett
All rights reserved.
Published 1970, by Beacon Press. Second printing
1973 by the Unitarian Universalist Association
Printed in the United States of America

CONTENTS

For Bill

CHAPTER ONE

A chunk of meat

The pink streaks of dawn sent the prowling leopards to the trees to sleep during the heat of the coming day. Soon the Kalahari Desert would bake in the hot sun of summer.

A herd of small antelope left its grassy bedding ground as the sky turned light. Quietly and gracefully the animals moved, wary for danger on the way to their morning drink at the water in the huge flat pan, a mile across but only an inch deep. Three *kudus,* heavy of shoulder and carrying their long twisted horns, lumbered to their feet to graze on their way to water.

In a camp of the Kung Bushmen an old man was the first to stir. Old Toma, his skin wrinkled with age and his eyes nearly blind, crept quietly from his small grass hut. Squatting by the ashes of last night's fire, he brushed the coals free to lay on some dry sticks. The warm flame licked up hungrily. He kept the fire small.

A moment later his wife flung aside the leather cape the two had used for a blanket. Old Khuana came and squatted beside him. She, too, was wrinkled. She, too, was old and nearly blind, though younger than Old Toma. Only dimly could they see beyond the campfire.

But they could tell by the sounds what was happening. Old Toma heard the quick excited chatter of the older boys. His keen ears recognized the voices of two of his grand-

9

children, Young Toma and Skinny Toma. He knew that the four older boys had slept at their own fire, away from home, a full fifty feet away from the nearest hut. He heard one boy talking about shooting a pair of doves. Then he heard the soft cooing of the doves and, suddenly, a whistle of wings as they flew. The other boys jeered at the one who had been too slow with his arrow.

With his mind's eye, Old Toma saw the many doves he had shot when he was a hunter. And he remembered the good meat that he had eaten. Meat was good. Nuts were all right. But meat was good. A hunter needed meat. Perhaps today he would eat meat.

His wife was dropping some nuts into the fire to roast for breakfast. Dimly Old Toma could see the practiced movements of the old woman, but his mind was on the other sounds of the camp. He heard the soft crackle of fires as other coals were fanned into flame. He heard the soft talking, the good-natured joking that always filled the camps of the Kung Bushmen. To his right he could hear the discussion of four men, preparing for the day's hunt. He heard them discussing the size of the kudu tracks which they had seen the afternoon before. He knew the voices, all four of them— three skilled hunters and a young man who had just made his first kill. One hunter was Toma's elder son, Slender Tekay.

And he heard other sounds. The children playing. One ran to his mother for a quick bit of nursing and affection. He heard a girl tell a child that he was old enough to go behind the bushes instead of wetting a puddle by the hut. And he heard the soft shushing sound of sand being kicked over the wet spot.

But Old Toma's mind was on meat. As he heard the four hunters stand to leave, he called a greeting to them. They laughed in response, assuring him that they would bring back meat tender enough even for his old toothless gums. And Old Toma joined in the laughter.

Dimly he saw them leave, walking toward the waterpan.

He knew that one might fill with water the empty shell of an ostrich egg he carried. And he knew, because he had done the same himself, that on the way each hunter would scan the ground for signs from the night before. They would see the tracks of the dainty duikers and the deep hoof marks of the great kudus. Perhaps they would see the wide *paw prints* of the leopard he had heard during the night.

In his mind he could see many of the events of their hunt. He could almost feel the soft wet ooze of the mud in the huge shallow pan of water. He remembered filling shells and plugging the holes with grass. He remembered walking miles through the sandy desert, now green with grass and rich with life. He knew how long they would walk in the heat of the rising sun. He knew the patience and skill that it took to make a kill. And then he thought of the meat that the hunters would bring home. Good meat.

Old Khuana had roasted the nuts. Expertly she flipped them out of the coals and divided them, half for Old Toma, half for herself. Yes, nuts were good, but his mind was on meat. He hoped that the hunters would get a kudu. One kudu would feed everyone in the camp for a week. It might weigh as much as five men.

As he chewed the nuts with what teeth he had left, Old Toma listened to the other sounds of the camp. He knew where each hut was. The children had eaten some nuts or roots. The women were preparing to work. They had tied their skin karosses over their yellow shoulders, carrying the small babies on their shoulders or in their arms or on their hips or tucked into the karosses. It was in these skin capes that the women would pack whatever roots and nuts and melons and berries they found today.

When the women had left, he heard the shouting boys depart in the opposite direction. They would spend all day looking for small game, for springhare, birds, and turtles. They would practice the patient art of stalking close enough to shoot. He remembered the years he had spent learning to hunt when he was young, so many, many winters ago.

The camp was quiet now. Old Toma sat on the ground by his tiny fire. He scraped an arrow shaft, needing only his sense of touch now to do what he had done so many times before in his long life. His wife sat beside him, serene with dignity. With endless patience she rolled fibers into string on her thigh. When the string was made she would tie it into net carrying bags, or her grandchildren might make some snares for birds.

Old Toma could feel the heat of the sun on his shoulders now as the rays slanted through the leaves of the camelthorn tree. Soon its heat would flame like an open fire piled too high with wood. This was the end of summer. This was the end of more summers than Old Toma could count. The heavy rains were over. It was a good time of year. The desert was green and in bloom. Food was easy.

But Old Toma knew that in two more full moons, the summer would be gone and so would autumn. Winter would come to the Kalahari as before. Winter would come with five months of dryness and cold winds that sucked up the water from the waterholes and shriveled the leaves. Winter would come to test the skill and endurance of all the men and animals who lived on the Kalahari.

All day the old couple kept at their work, patiently rolling fibers, patiently fashioning arrows. They felt the flaming sun pass overhead, beating on their heads like a hammer. They moved about only to get another tool or to pick up another stick or more fiber. They talked in low voices about their children and their children's children. They talked of the children to come.

In late afternoon the women returned, shouting cheerfully from the distance. He knew from the glad sound of their voices that their skin capes were bulging with food, packed with melons and berries, roots and nuts. But Old Toma's mind was on the hunters. A dozen times that day in his imagination he had seen them kill a giant kudu. A dozen times he had cooked a huge chunk of the meat in his fire. As the women came, he called out greetings. The children ran to him, climbing on his shoulders. He patted and kissed them affectionately. The camp was bustling with activity. Fires were tended, roots cleaned and pounded, nuts cracked open.

The boys returned. Proudly they carried home two springhares and a porcupine.

Then the hunters came. They had failed to get the kudu. But they did have two *steenboks*. Joking and laughter filled the air as the men recited in detail their hunt and their kill.

Old Toma joined in the joking. Soon one of the hunters came over with a gift for the old man, a chunk of meat from one of the small antelope. Food was shared in the band.

The odor of cooking meat pleased Old Toma. He joined in teasing the hunters for missing the kudu. He heard their plans for the next day. Then Old Toma called one of the hunters to him. He gave him an arrow, the arrow he had worked on most of the day. As Giver of the Arrow, Old Toma would receive a big share of the animal it killed.

The sun set slowly, flaming red on the underside of the clouds in the west. One of the hunters strummed music on his hunting bow, beating the string with a twig. He sang a song about hunting the giant kudu but killing only a tiny steenbok. The younger children crawled into their huts to sleep. Babies nursed at their mothers' breasts. Fires died to coals. Slowly the camp settled to quiet. Old Toma, listening, placed each hut, identified each voice.

The last voice he heard was that of Tsamgao, the young husband of his granddaughter. Smiling Khuana was heavy with her first child, and Old Toma knew that as the young woman lay on the grass in the arms of her husband, the coming birth was much upon her mind. He knew that she lay there, half in tenderness for her husband and half in fear of the spirits of the dark. Soon, perhaps tonight or to-morrow, her baby would come, and when her baby came she must leave the camp and go out alone to give birth. And in the dark the spirits came close to the fire. The spirits were dangerous.

Old Toma prayed to the God of the West that his first great-grandchild would be born safely.

13

The flames had died. Each woman had covered the coals with ashes before crawling into her hut to sleep. Old Toma and his wife lay on one skin and covered themselves with another. In the distance they heard the cough of a hunting leopard. Then the camp slept.

Above the camp the stars gleamed. High above the sleeping Bushmen, high above the Kalahari Desert, high above the great southern bulge of Africa, high above the slowly turning earth, the stars glittered in the black night sky.

Two walks and two sleeps

Slender Tekay led his family through the cold sands of the desert. In single file the family walked barefoot through the stiff and yellow head-high grass, through the scattered bushes, toward the giant *baobab* tree on the horizon. Behind Slender Tekay came the other hunter in the family, his daughter's husband, Tsamgao. Next came his daughter, Smiling Khuana, who carried his three-year-old grandson, too tired to walk. Slender Tekay's two other children followed behind her. His wife Nai brought up the rear. The two women each had a skin kaross stuffed with ostrich egg shells filled with water slung over her back. Each man carried a pole over his shoulder with a sack hanging from each end. A spear on the other shoulder took some of the weight.

They were walking to their food. The family was on a walk to the forest of mongongo nut trees that grew on a high reddish sand dune a full day's walk away. Their food lay on the ground under the mongongo nut trees far ahead. But their water lay in a tiny waterhole far behind them where the rest of the band was camped.

15

To eat they must walk for many miles through the dry and wintry desert. They must carry enough water for both the trip out and the trip back to the permanent waterhole. To

live, they needed both food and water. To live they must carry water to the food and then carry food back to the water. Again and again through the hungry season of Gaw, the family had made such marches. For three months they had walked for their food, farther and farther each month.

Slender Tekay had planned this trip carefully. Tonight they would make camp at the great forest of mongongo nut trees. In the morning, with almost half of their water gone, they would gather hundreds of nuts in their huge skin karosses and eat nuts till they were stuffed. Then they would drink more of their precious water to lighten the load. After one more sleep, they would have only a day's walking left to reach home. If all went well, they could make the journey in three days, two of walking and one of gathering, and with only two sleeps.

Slender Tekay had made such a trip for many of these seasons of hunger and thirst which the Bushmen called the season of Gaw. In the Kalahari Desert Gaw meant cold nights, hot days, dry winds, and thirst. In the cold nights the Bushmen needed food and fire to keep warm. In the dry, rainless winter, the shallow waterpans had dried to mud flats. They had to remain close to their few permanent deep water-holes, spots of green in the yellow desert.

For Slender Tekay Gaw was one season among many. He had lived through many cycles of seasons. He knew that even the coldest and driest winter would pass. It was always followed by rains. The rains would come.

And when the rains came the grass turned green. Bushes pushed out green leaves. Flowers bloomed. Water collected in those waterholes that had been dry all winter. The spring rains of Hooma, Slender Tekay called them. Rains sent new life into the withered vines and plants that had endured the dry winter by using up the moisture stored in large underground roots. During the spring rains Slender Tekay's family could relax.

After the spring rains of Hooma, came the heavy summer rains of Bara. Torrents poured down. From December to March great storm clouds dumped rain on the Kalahari

17

Desert. The scrawny shelters of grass and branches that the women built offered little protection. Rain leaked through. Rain put out fires. Rain, warm rain, fell on their yellow-brown shoulders. Rain filled all the waterholes. It overflowed in huge flat pans of water a mile wide and lip deep. Herds of *eland* and kudu and wildebeest and hartebeest drank the water and grazed on the green grass. The heavy rains of Bara, the warm, wet summer on the desert, gave food and strength to endure the winter. The rains renewed life.

During the season of Bara, the Bushmen ate the meat of the eland and the kudu and the other great antelope. They hunted the little springbok and the duiker and the steenbok. And they killed many wart hogs. The women gathered berries and sour plums and melons. During the season of Bara everyone ate well. They ate meat. The strong young hunters would stalk the horned antelope with their poisoned arrows. And when they brought home the meat, it was shared with all the camp. Everyone ate. And they ate almost everything but the bones and horns and the gall bladder.

After Bara, the rains lessened and stopped. Water gleamed silently in the huge flat pans. Lions and leopards drank there at night, and the great herds of antelope came in the day. Slender Tekay's family moved camp often in this season. It was a time for visiting, the season of Obay, the warm days of autumn. It was a time of plenty and of good water. It was a time to visit kin and to give gifts and to talk and to dance. For an older boy it was a good time to kill his first antelope, permitting him to undergo the Ceremony of the First Kill. Only thus could he become a man. Only then could he marry.

But the warm dry days of Obay soon dried up the flat pans of water, leaving mud flats, dry and cracked. The small ponds dried out. Much of the game moved out of the desert far away into wetter lands. Then the Bushmen camped near their permanent waterholes. At night the winter winds began to chill the air. Water standing overnight in a turtle shell or in an empty melon froze to ice. The families huddled closer to their fires for warmth. The dry cold of the season they called Goom was upon them. It was the season of winter, the months of May, June, July, and August.

Worse even than winter was winter's end, the season called Gaw, the bitterest time of the year. During the three months of Gaw the nights were still cold, but the days turned hot and dry. The sun sucked the moisture from the leaves and from the ground, drying up all the water. Even in the permanent waterholes, the level dropped low. The women found that they had gathered all the berries and melons and dug up all the roots near camp. Each day they had to roam farther and farther for food. Game was scarce. The hunters usually returned empty-handed. Gaw was the bitter time. It was a time that a Bushman might die of hunger and thirst. It was the season that kept away those other men who once had stolen the greener lands from the Bushmen. Only because of the thirst of the desert did the Bushmen live in the Kalahari seldom troubled by the Bantu and the whites who had stolen their richer lands and driven them to hide in the Kalahari. For the land of the yellow Bushmen was the land that the white men and the black men did not want.

Slender Tekay did not know of the land or the peoples beyond the desert. He could not know of the huge continent to the north called Africa of which his desert was a small part. He could not even dream of as much water as lay in the Atlantic Ocean far to the west. But he did know the seasons within the Kalahari. He had lived through many of them. He had walked barefoot over many miles of desert, just as he was walking now.

A sudden cry from his daughter stopped them all. Smiling Khuana pointed at the sky, the sky which had been blue and empty for months. Far to the west a cloud, a white cloud, was drifting slowly above the horizon. Perhaps the first rains of spring would come soon. They walked on with new hope surging inside each heart. Spring was coming. The rains were coming, the life-giving rains.

When they crossed a dry river bed, they could imagine it brimming with rain. As soon as they returned from their nut gathering, they might have a Rain Dance to celebrate.

19

CHAPTER THREE

The first kill

Young Toma squatted on his heels by Old Toma's fire. Across the tiny blaze, his grandfather lay on the sand propped on one elbow. Fat Gunda crawled over the old man's thin legs and snuggled in beside him to listen.

Young Toma teased his young cousin. "Come, great hunter, what meat did you bring me today?"

The five-year-old boy stared up solemnly. Then his face crinkled into a laugh as he turned to the old man, who was his great-grandfather. Old Toma patted him and continued the tale of his First Kill. He was barely fourteen then, the same age as the eager young hunter across the fire.

That had been many years ago. Old Toma was then called Tall Toma. In those days *arrowheads* were all made of sharpened bone instead of bits of iron and steel from the white traders, or taken from the fences of the white farmers. The old man's eyes, nearly blind now, had been keen then. He had been tireless in running and expert at tracking. And at the age of fourteen he had made his First Kill. A giant kudu buck. As he told Young Toma the story, he rubbed the thin black lines on his right arm. Three lines of scars, three horizontal tattoos on his right arm, showed that he had killed a male antelope. His next kill, two moons later,

21

had been a female, and then he had earned the scars on his left arm.

The two boys listened, the five year old in interest and delight, his fourteen-year-old cousin with mounting eagerness. Young Toma's eyes shone as he imagined himself making his First Kill.

For Young Toma was ready. He had been practicing for three years to become a hunter. His days were filled with tracking and stalking and running. He had killed many small animals for practice. His nights were filled with tales of the hunt and in dreams of hunting. He wanted to be a skillful hunter, as skillful as Tall Kwee, his father, and as tireless as Old Toma, his grandfather, had been. Young Toma wanted to become a man; he wanted to do a man's work.

Abruptly Fat Gunda left his great-grandfather. Young Toma watched him circle the fire and walk to his mother at her fire four paces away. The boy took his mother's breast to nurse quietly for a minute while his mother patted him affectionately with one hand and kept on with her business of roasting nuts.

Young Toma watched as the boy left his mother and went into the grass hut to find his tiny bow and his arrow made of a long thorn. In a minute he emerged to go hunting. He was searching for caterpillars. With exaggerated caution, he searched through the leaves of one bush, then another. At last he found a large beetle. He crept close, thorn on the string, bow bending as he pulled it. He poked the thorn so close to the *beetle* that he almost pierced the beetle before he released the thorn. Proudly he brought back his wriggling prize to Young Toma who patted and praised him.

Young Toma could recall hunting beetles and caterpillars. He could recall his childhood in camp after camp. He remembered living in the same hut with his mother and father. Not until he was ten years old did he leave that hut and move to the older boys' hut with their own fire.

The older boys were almost men. They were getting ready to put aside the play of little boys and to adopt the duties of men, the serious business of hunting.

The five-year-old had more years of play, of being carried and of being pampered and loved. He would soon stop nursing, but no one demanded that he work. When he was older he would demand of himself that he hunt.

The boy would go through the same stages that Young Toma had gone through, of playing with the older boys, of drifting further and further away from his parents, of playing games that strengthened his legs and sharpened his skills. He would play janee with the boys, throwing a birdlike toy up in the air with a stick and catching it before it touched the ground. Janee meant a lot of running. There were no boundaries to the game, only the desert.

And as Young Toma grew up, he had silently absorbed the right ways of doing things. He had learned to point, not rudely with his fingers, but politely with the lips. He had learned that you shared food and never let a person in the camp go hungry. You gave food to your close kin and they shared it with others.

He had learned the right way to behave. A baby boy might urinate where he stood, but an older boy learned to go behind the bushes or in the tall grass. And the boys learned to keep the skin *garment* tied between their legs to cover the penis which on all Bushmen boys and men stands partly stiff throughout their lives.

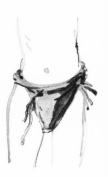

He had learned that some relatives joked with him while others did not, and that he could joke back only with those who joked with him. He had learned that men always sit on the left of the fire as you face away from the hut.

For four years Young Toma had lived with the older boys. He had shot doves and snared many birds. He had killed springhare in their tunnels, hooking them out with a long flexible stick. He had crept up close to many small duikers or steenboks and then, rising to shoot, had seen the nervous animals dash away. But Young Toma had learned to be patient and silent so that when he again crept up close to the duikers or steenboks, he had hit them with his arrows. And he had proudly brought the meat home to his parents. Now he was the oldest of the boys.

23

Always Young Toma had dreamed of the big kill, his first big kill—a kudu or an eland or some other large animal. As he had gained in skill and strength and endurance and patience, the older men had permitted him to join them on their hunts. But when the crucial moment came, it was always an older man who launched that deadly arrow. Meat was too important to risk losing it. Always Young Toma had watched and learned. He had imitated the tricks of crawling and of testing the wind with a pinch of dust. You must hunt upwind, so the nervous and wary antelope will not smell you.

Always Young Toma dreamed of his First Kill.

And then three days later, his chance came.

He was out with two other boys hunting for duiker, the little rabbit-sized antelope with the spiky horns. In his *quiver* rested two poisoned arrows, ready, waiting for the big chance.

They had spotted the track of some duikers. They had trailed them carefully, noiselessly, patiently. They had located the tiny animals in a grassy clearing near some thorn bushes and had crept up quietly with Young Toma in the lead.

When he saw the *duikers,* Young Toma decided to leave all his hunting gear on the ground, advancing only with a bow and arrow. And then, suddenly, grandly, out stepped an eland. Young Toma was so close that he could see the thin white stripes on the animal's brown hide. The eland bent her neck to graze.

Young Toma's fingers almost trembled as he selected the poisoned arrow. He notched it and crept up quietly, moving when the eland's head was down, freezing when the eland lifted her head under those short, straight horns.

Under his breath, Young Toma prayed. He prayed to the God of the West, the Lesser God.

Help me that I kill this animal.
Help me. I am hungry.
Help me to kill this animal.
Help me to make my First Kill.

Then with infinite patience and caution, he crawled closer. When the eland's head bent down once more, Young Toma rose to his knee, drew the bow, aimed, and shot, all in one smooth, practiced motion.

The deadly arrow plunged into the soft side of the eland's belly. The eland snorted, leaped, and crashed through the thorn bushes, running fast.

Young Toma scarcely remembered the rest of the day. He knew that the three boys, pulsing with excitement, ran across the desert, following the trail. He knew that he ran faster than he had ever run before, faster than he should run in case it was a two-day chase.

He remembered that they ran all that afternoon. Twice they had caught up with the eland only to see her dash away again. At last they had come upon the dying animal and they had killed her with a spear. Young Toma had sent the youngest boy back to the camp with the news. He and the other boy made a fire for the night and began to skin the giant beast.

In the morning the men came. Young Toma's father, Tall Kwee, walked rapidly in the lead, proud of his son. They carried the meat back near the camp, stopping where the women could not see them.

Tall Kwee kindled a fire. Young Toma boiled water in a pot and into this pot Tall Kwee dropped bits of meat cut from the eland: bits from the chest, the foreleg, the back, and the ear. He also put in one eye. Then Kwee charred some medicine root in the fire and mixed it with the froth bubbling on the stew to make a black paste. Separately he mixed some froth with eland blood to make a red paste. Then Kwee ceremoniously ate one piece of meat from the pot.

Next Kwee selected a new arrow from his quiver, an arrow that had never been poisoned. Young Toma stood up straight and tall and proud before his father. Kwee pinched the skin above Toma's left elbow and with the sharp tip of the arrow scratched a tiny vertical cut into the skin. A dozen cuts he scratched, then a dozen more. The blood oozed out slowly. Young Toma never blinked. Into the shallow cuts Kwee rubbed the black paste. Then he rubbed in the red paste. The many vertical cuts formed one strong horizontal tattoo.

"May you have strong arms, my son. May you have strong arms for shooting arrows and hurling spears."

Kwee cut two more tattoos higher up on Toma's left arm. Then he cut two more on the left side of Toma's chest. He rubbed in the black paste, then the red.

"May you have strong lungs, my son. You will need strong lungs for running after the kill. May you have a strong heart that sends you out hunting after meat."

Kwee scratched another line of cuts on the back of Toma's left shoulder to keep an animal from turning its head to see the hunter.

Last, Kwee cut a row of tiny cuts on his son's forehead. He rubbed in the black paste, and then the red.

"May you see well, my son. May you have keen eyes to see the game and to shoot straight."

The unused bits of black and red paste were hidden under a bush where no woman would step on it. Quietly the other men ate the stew from the pot. They divided up the meat of the huge eland among those who had fathered three children. Only such men could eat meat from a First Kill. Young Toma and his father could not eat it, for that would spoil Young Toma's hunting.

The cuts would heal. They would remain as a row of tiny, black scars. They were the tattoos of a man, the badge of honor. His scars showed to all the world that Young Toma was now a hunter, a grown man, ready to marry, ready to assume responsibility.

This was the Ceremony of his First Kill.

CHAPTER FOUR

Nutcrackers and digging sticks

Nai carried her digging stick in her right hand. With her left she balanced a pole slung on her left shoulder. At each end of the pole hung a bag that swayed as she walked. Ahead of her walked the other women caped in animal skin from shoulder to ankle. And ahead of them walked the children. The men of the band led the way, their naked backs yellow-brown in the wintry sun.

Nai carried all her possessions. In her *kaross* bulging behind her were all of her eight ostrich egg shells now filled with water. The two sacks that bent the pole with their weight held her other belongings. In the front sack she had pieces of soft skin, an extra kaross rolled into a bundle, and a roll of strong cord made by her mother-in-law, Old Khuana. In her other bag she carried her wooden mortar and pounding stick, several carved wooden paddles, wooden spoons, and wooden bowls, and a small skin bag stuffed with all the extra food available—some dried meat, tsi beans, and a few dozen

mongongo nuts. She wore her beads around her neck and tied to her hair.

Her husband, Slender Tekay, led the walk. He knew every sand dune, every valley, every waterhole for miles and miles in every direction. Now he was headed for another waterhole for the second winter camp. Tekay guided them almost straight across the desert to the water, heading a bit to the east because he knew where food was available. The rest of their band would follow later.

Thirteen Bushmen made up this small group. The rest of the band had decided to stay at their first winter camp for a few days more. For most of the year the band size was nearly thirty members. But as the winter wore on the band often split into smaller units. Tekay and Tall Kwee, the two brothers, had camped together ever since they had returned from bride service, and their families and parents made up this small unit.

Old Toma walked behind Tekay. Old Toma was headman still despite his failing eyes, but Tekay made most of the decisions. It was Tekay who led, Tekay who selected the campsite, Tekay who usually led the hunts. But always he spoke in the name of Toma. Always he deferred to the authority of his father, the headman.

Tall Kwee came right behind his father. Like his brother Tekay, Kwee carried a pole on his left shoulder with a sack at each end. And on his right shoulder he carried a spear. The tip of the spear had been thrust under the pole to carry some of the weight of the sacks. On his back hung a quiver of arrows and a bow.

Nai saw all these things in one glance. She also saw that her son-in-law Tsamgao had picked up his child to carry. It was Fat Gunda whose tiny legs could seldom walk very far. Now he rode high on his father's shoulders, clutching one handful of hair and smiling proudly at the world.

Nai's younger children, Skinny Toma and Naoka, carried their own burdens. So did Kwee's children, Young Toma and Young Khuana. The big cousins, both named Toma, teased each other as they walked. Nai smiled indulgently at their joking.

The women brought up the rear of the line. Directly behind the children came Smiling Khuana, Nai's daughter. Old Khuana, after whom both of the younger women were named, came next, sturdily bearing her load. Then came Ungka, wife of Kwee, and last was Nai.

As Nai walked at the end of the line, her eyes roved restlessly over the ground looking for signs of food. She had spent all of her life looking for the leaf which marked a root that could be eaten, for the dried stem that revealed a supply of water bulging in an underground root, for the dead leaf that showed where the *tsama* melons grew, for the bushes of the berries she loved so well, or for the big trees of the mongongo nut forests. Nai knew every bush and tree by sight and by name and by use.

On her left she saw the valley which she and Ungka and Young Khuana had scoured only a few days ago. They had been looking for tsi beans and had found many of them. Each had carried her kaross home full.

Ahead and a bit to the right she saw where they had dug edible roots, shoveling the dirt and rocks with their digging sticks. And here was a hole where the boys had dug out a springhare.

For two moons Nai's family had camped in that valley, roaming farther and farther each week as they had eaten the better food near camp. Plenty of food could still be found within easy walking distance. But the best food was gone. The tasty nuts, the favorite tsi beans, and the best roots were all eaten. So once more Tekay led half the band to a new camp, a new home by a waterhole for the rest of the season of Gaw.

As Tekay topped a small sand dune, his eyes caught sight of the landmark toward which he had been aiming. A huge baobab tree towered above all the other trees and brush. A few more miles and they would be there. The stop had been planned. It would give them time to gather food and time to make a temporary camp.

When they reached the baobab tree the sun was already far to the west, only the width of two hands above the horizon. Over them the huge tree towered into the sky. Nai thought that if the entire group of thirteen were to hold hands, they could not encircle that mighty trunk.

Young Toma was pleading with his father. He wanted to climb the baobab tree. The first limb was thirty feet above Toma's head, but a line of wooden *pegs* had been hammered into the soft wood of the trunk. Toma climbed while the rest of the band set to work gathering fallen fruit. Nai could see on his arm the black scars from the Ceremony of the First Kill.

They picked and chose among the baobab fruit, for it spoiled quickly once it was on the ground. Soon all were squatting on the ground, chewing the pulp which was sticky and cool and sweet. They spat out the seeds, then took another bite of the sticky pulp.

High above them Toma was eating the pick of the fruit. Skinny Toma yelled to him and soon Young Toma was tossing fresh fruit down from the limbs of the great baobab.

While there still was light, Nai set to work gathering firewood, urging the children to pick up more fruit to eat by the firelight.

Nai did not make a hut. The evening was not very cold. Instead she thrust two branches into the ground to indicate where the hut entrance would be so that she and Tekay knew where to sit. In front of the branches she laid her fire, keeping a few extra sticks at hand for later. Behind her upright branches she scooped out a shallow spot in the sand and pulled up great handfuls of grass to spread for softness and warmth. Over this she spread one kaross, keeping the other for a blanket for herself and Tekay.

Old Toma and Tekay squatted facing each other to make the fire with Old Toma's firesticks. Soon four fires were burning: Nai's fire, Ungka's fire, Old Khuana's fire, and Smiling Khuana's fire where Fat Gunda nursed contentedly at his mother's breast. The boys did not bother to build a separate fire; they usually ate at their parents' fire, and this one night they could sleep there as well.

They ate more fruit. Some roasted tsi beans and mongongo nuts in the fires. The murmur of conversation drifted over the campsite. Bantering jokes were called back and forth.

Shortly after sunset all were asleep and the fires were barely glowing under the protective ashes.

By sunrise they were up in the cool morning air. Nai quickly repacked. All of the women gathered as much of the baobab fruit as they could carry. In a few moments they were on the trail again. Fat Gunda rode happily on his mother's shoulder.

All day Nai followed the single file of walkers led by her husband. To an outsider the dry scrub of the desert would have seemed trackless and all alike. But to Slender Tekay and Kwee the hills had distinctive shapes. The valleys were places they had been before. The ground was covered with tracks both new and old.

Nai knew the land also. But she had not hunted as Tekay had, nor ranged as far from camp. Yet she had walked this trail many times as the band shifted from waterhole to waterhole.

On the afternoon of the second day Nai knew that they were getting close to the end of the trail. Tekay had quickened his pace ever so slightly, and she knew he could now sight where they were going.

Tekay led them up to the crest of a small dune covered with brush and trees. He stopped. Below them, perhaps five times as far as a man could shoot an arrow, was the green spot of a waterhole. In the golden grass and the brown-leaved shrubs, the green reeds seemed a patch of summer. By camping so far away they would not frighten the animals from the water.

This waterhole would become their new home. Day by day the women would collect the tastiest food in ever-widen-
ing circles, although sometimes Tekay would plan a three-day trip: one day out, one day of gathering mongongo nuts, and one day to return.

Tekay had walked right past the campsite where they had lived last year. A campsite is never used twice. He selected another spot, put down his load, and Nai knew immediately where her fire and her hut would be. Old Toma was led to the spot Tekay had picked for him. In moments the entire band was busy. Children gathered mongongo nuts. The men hung their bows and their quivers of poisoned arrows high on branches. The women built huts.

Nai wandered through the grove breaking off long curved branches. When she had several dozen about eight feet or more long, she carried them back to her site and set to work building a house.

With her *digging stick* Nai loosened the earth in a crescent-shaped series of holes. She placed the thick butt end of each stick in a hole, and then tamped the earth solidly around each stick to hold it in place. The slender ends of the branches curved toward the top center, and these she twisted together, interlacing them. Next she gathered bundles of grass and thatched the hut to keep out the winds of winter, the cold winds of Gaw which soon would be upon them.

In front of the hut Nai laid her fire, leaning small twigs against a log. She did not light it yet.

Smiling Khuana's hut was behind the one that Nai had built. Old Khuana's was just to the right. Old Khuana had prepared a fire, but it was not yet burning. But farther away Old Toma, with the help of Slender Tekay, was building the new fire.

From his sack Old Toma had taken his *firesticks*. One was flat with notches and holes in it. The other was smooth and round, a long slender spindle. Old Toma had twigs ready and a handful of dry grass for tinder. He placed the notched board on the grass and twirled the spindle on it. With the flat of his palms pressing the spindle, he spun the stick to make heat by friction.

One man could make fire this way, but two could make it faster. Slender Tekay squatted facing his father and placed his hands above those of Old Toma. Down he pressed, twirling as fast as he could. Then Toma's hands were at the top and the two men alternately worked their hands down the spindle, spinning and spinning.

A curl of smoke, a spark, and then the grass burst into flame. Quickly Toma lay twigs on the flame and built it up with larger and larger branches.

Old Toma laid some tsi beans and mongongo nuts in the fire. He prayed.

God of the West, keep evil away from this camp.
Keep sickness and death away from this camp.

The New Fire blazed up. Old Toma called that the New Fire was ready. Tekay carried a burning branch back to the fire Nai had made ready. Smiling Khuana came to get a torch. Ungka carried one to her site. Young Toma and Skinny Toma came over for New Fire. And then Old Toma carried the last torch over to the hut where he and Old Khuana were to live. The rest of the New Fire burned out.

Nai had finished her hut and laid a mattress of dry grass inside. All of her belongings were neatly stored in the hut and near the fire where she could reach them. Nai was an efficient housekeeper.

As soon as that work was done, Nai slipped out into the dusk to gather mongongo nuts for the evening meal. When her kaross bulged sufficiently, she headed back for the camp-site of last year. For there, under a spreading tree where she had once built a hut, lay two stones, her *nutcrackers*.

There they were, a small hammerstone resting on a large flat stone. She carried them to her hut balanced on one hip so that she could also drag a dead tree for firewood.

Nai had built her hut in one hour. She gathered food for several meals and wood for two days in the next hour.

Tomorrow the three wives and the children would gather more food. The men would hunt. The boys would hunt. Old Toma and Old Khuana would stay in camp.

Nai squatted by the fire next to Slender Tekay, her husband. She felt comfortable in her usual place to the right of the fire in front of her hut with the bed already made inside it. Her wooden mortar and pounding stick stood nearby. Her ostrich egg shells were lined neatly against a dead log. Her children were nearby. Once more Nai was at home.

CHAPTER FIVE

Until the third child

After Young Toma had made his First Kill, he hoped to get married. He did not need to seek a wife. His father, Tall Kwee, and his mother, Ungka, had selected a wife for him years before, when he was about six.

Before he had grown big enough to leave their hut to sleep with the older boys, Toma's mother and father had made plans. Kwee's brother, Slender Tekay, had a wife, Nai, whose brother Namshi had a daughter named Naoka. At this time Naoka was less than a year old. The parents of Toma talked with the parents of Naoka and the matter was arranged.

Kwee and Ungka had no knowledge of what kind of a girl young Naoka would grow into. But they knew her parents, and they reasoned that the girl would grow up somewhat like her mother. Her mother, Shama, was a fine-looking woman, pleasant, and she kept a neat house. She dug roots every day regardless of weather. She always picked a good spot for her hut, and she laid her *ostrich egg shells* in neat rows where she could reach them from the fire and she seldom broke any. She did not wander away from her fire at night to visit. When you sat down by her fire you found that the sand had been swept and brushed free of any thorns. Yes, if Naoka grew up to be like her mother, then Young Toma would be fortunate.

On the other hand, Shama and Namshi felt that Young Toma would be a good husband for their daughter. Wasn't he the son of Tall Kwee, one of the best hunters around? Often they had eaten meat shared by Tall Kwee from one of his many kills.

Namshi was a good hunter himself. And he knew that Tall Kwee was skillful and generous. He did not want his daughter to marry a man who came from a "far-hearted" family where the courtesies of sharing were not common. Certainly he did not want her to marry a lazy man from a lazy family.

Namshi had a real reason for considering Young Toma's hunting ability. When the two young people married, Young Toma would move near to Namshi's hut. He would perform bride service for Namshi. He would hunt and hunt and hunt, and much of the meat would come to Naoka and to Namshi and Shama. For years Young Toma would hunt for his father-in-law. He would stay until Naoka had given birth to three children. He would help with the hunting while Young Geishay, Naoka's older brother, was far away performing his bride service.

Namshi and Shama loved to eat meat and the addition of a skilled hunter to the family was important. For Namshi's father, Old Geishay, had been a mighty hunter. So skillful had Old Geishay been that he had taken a second wife. First he married Naoka. Then he married her younger sister, Gisa. Over the course of many years Naoka had become Old Naoka and Gisa had become Old Gisa. But always Old Geishay had hunted well. He had been a skillful tracker, better than most. He had been a tireless runner, better than most. He made straight arrows that hit their target.

Now he was too old to hunt, but he still made the best arrows. He made them and gave them to the younger men to shoot. Then they repaid him with a big gift of meat. For the Giver of the Arrow always gets a big share of meat. Meat is good.

Thus Young Toma's destiny had been planned for him for many years. His parents had made the choice. They knew the ancient customs, and by the time Toma was old enough to get married, he knew them also. He could not marry his sister or his mother, nor a woman who was like a sister or a mother. Toma knew he could not marry aunts, nieces, stepsisters, halfsisters, or cousins. In fact, he could not marry most of the women who lived in his own band. The ancient customs also cut out a lot of other women not in the band, but Toma's choice had been made for him. He never gave it another thought. Accepting Naoka as his future wife was like accepting the rains of summer and the winds of winter. They just came. His wife was waiting.

Both sets of parents wanted their children well married. For Namshi and Shama it meant that for ten or fifteen years Toma and his wife and their children would live in the same band. And for Tall Kwee and Ungka it meant that ten or fifteen years after the wedding, Toma would return with his wife and family and would probably help Kwee to hunt. By then Kwee would be older, and having a strong young hunter in the family would be insurance for plenty of meat. By then Young Geishay would return to hunt for Namshi.

The engagement was agreed upon. Shama gave Ungka a long string of white *shell beads*. Ungka gave Shama some copper wire.

Toma was fifteen when he became eligible to marry. Once he had earned the scars on his arm for making his First Kill, he was ready to wed. But first he must kill another antelope and present it as a gift to Namshi, his future father-in-law.

But hunting was bad. For many changes of the moon the hunting was bad. Toma killed small animals. He shot duikers and guinea fowl. He brought home dozens of spring-hare. Once he even shot an ostrich. But the big antelope that he must present to Naoka's father did not come his way.

The big antelope did not come the way of any of the older hunters, either. Then during the early spring rains when the grass was just beginning to grow green again, Toma killed a kudu.

He killed it a two days' walk away from camp. And the

camp of Naoka and her father, Namshi, was a three days' walk away.

The young man with Toma helped him. They cut the meat up and the friend stayed to guard it while Toma ran to Namshi's camp for help. He ran most of the way and then ran back. He made the round trip in three days.

Namshi came, too, smiling and proud of this strong young man. They hauled the meat away and had a feast, and Namshi gave great chunks of meat to his relatives and friends.

A few weeks later the rains brought green to the desert. Food became more abundant. Herds of antelope moved in for grazing on the land that now flourished.

Kwee and Ungka, at Toma's urging, decided to visit the camp of Namshi and Shama.

Very quickly the wedding was arranged. Naoka was only a child of ten. She looked up with pride at this handsome young hunter who brought meat and who could run so well.

The next day the two women, Shama and Ungka, built a *wedding hut*. They gathered the branches and set them firmly into the ground. They gathered bunches of grass and tied them into neat bundles. This was to be a special hut. The branches were longer than usual. They even tied the thatch on with string lest the wind blow it away.

Naoka watched them working. She sat on a kaross so she would not touch the ground. She kept another kaross over her head so the sun would not touch her.

At sunset two of Naoka's girl relatives came over to her to conduct her to the wedding hut. Naoka refused to go. Laughing and giggling, the two girls seized her and carried her wrapped in the kaross to the hut. Her feet did not touch the ground. They laid her inside. She said nothing the rest of the evening.

39

Firewood was lying in front of the hut. The two mothers, Ungka and Shama, each carried a flaming torch from her own fire. Together they lighted the new fire for the

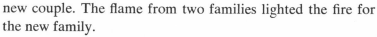

new couple. The flame from two families lighted the fire for the new family.

Meanwhile Young Toma had been sitting quietly by the older boy's fire. He pretended to ignore the whole ritual, but actually he was watching carefully. Then the other boys dragged him to the wedding hut. Toma pretended to resist a little. All of the boys sat near the fire except Toma who sat behind them, not talking, not singing, not eating.

One of the boys strummed on a bow. Then another boy appeared with a *guashee,* a more complicated instrument with strings tied to pegs. For hours the group sat and sang songs. Two of the boys roasted nuts in the fire and ate them. Another cooked a piece of meat and ate it.

The older people ignored them. For them, the ceremony was over with the lighting of the new fire.

As the fires burned down, the young people left the new couple to themselves. Toma slept outside his bride's hut.

At sunrise he was up and off for the hunt. He wanted to prove that he was a good hunter, a man.

Shama came over to see her daughter. She brought over some fat saved from the last big animal killed. With the fat she rubbed Naoka's body till it glistened. Using a reddish powder stored in a hollow reed, she painted designs on her daughter. On each cheek she painted a circle. On her forehead she painted a stripe.

When the women left for the day's digging, the ten-year-old picked up her digging stick and went to dig. Her childish playing was over. That night she cooked the roots she had gathered for her husband, and she cooked the meat he brought home. And Namshi gave Young Toma a gift, a beautifully cured gemsbok kaross.

The wedding of Naoka and Toma followed ancient Bushman customs. First marriages were arranged by the parents. Later marriages were arranged by the man and woman involved.

None of the hunters in either Toma's band or Naoka's band had more than one wife. Only Old Geishay, Namshi's father, had two wives. But since he had been the best hunter around, it was considered appropriate. Old Naoka had made no fuss over having her younger sister come as a second wife.

Some wives fuss. They may drive a young girl away with abuse and nagging. That is one reason why men say that it is wise to marry two sisters. Sisters are already adjusted to each other; they can get along.

Once Namshi told young Naoka a story about the three stars in the sky (which some people call the belt of Orion). Namshi said that the three stars were three zebras. The male slept in the middle and had a wife on each side to keep him warm. The stars reminded him of Old Geishay, his father.

Most men cannot support two wives. The first wife becomes jealous and manages to discourage the taking of a second wife.

Very few hunters are skillful enough to keep one small family well fed. There is no way for them to store food or to collect wealth. Meat is shared. Beads are given. Even a knife or a spear is given to someone who needs it or who shows an interest in it. Nobody has great wealth; nobody is poorer than others. Prestige comes from giving, not from having. A man can make only two investments in the future. One is to make arrows and, as Giver of the Arrow, receive a share of the kill each time someone uses one of his arrows.

The other investment in the future is to have daughters who will bring strong young hunters home for bride service or sons who will return from bride service to hunt meat for the father in his old age.

Men are proud to give away meat. Very early a boy learns to respect the hunter skillful enough to bring home a big kill to share with others. The boy sees the respect paid to the rare hunter strong enough to keep two wives and wants to become a great hunter himself.

That is the way most learning is done with the Kung. Children see examples all about them. That is the way they prepare for marriage. They learn about sex behavior by sleeping in a tiny hut with their mother and father. They accept their parents' loving and embracing as normally and as casually as they accept the cuddling and kissing that the Kung shower on their babies.

The children are right there in the hut. Also they can observe the mating of wild animals. They may see a bull kudu mount a cow. Or they might observe jackals mating, or hyenas. And with the alert mimicry of the Kung, the boys will act out what they have seen. It is not done as a joke, just as play. More importantly, it is learning.

Most of such learning occurs easily. The parents do not speak of sex; they are too modest. But sex is accepted casually. Thus, when boys are old enough, sex activity comes as no shock. It begins in their sleep, as it does for boys all over the world. Suddenly one night it will happen. The boy has a vivid dream of mating, of acting as he has seen his father act, of acting as he has seen the kudu bull act.

Kung boys sleep apart from their families at adolescence. In all parts of the world boys tease each other and play with each other. The Kung are no different. And the play is part of their learning about sex.

Boys grow up wishing to become great hunters able to keep two wives. Very few manage to become skilled enough. The few who take two wives still follow the marriage customs. A man performs bride service for his second wife also. Together the two periods of bride service may take many years, unless, like Geishay, the man marries a sister of his wife and his two periods of bride service overlap.

Marriages are not always happy. As in other parts of the world, husbands get angry. Wives run away. When the strain is too great, the couple divorces by separating. It is very simple. There is no ceremony. They simply agree to separate. No property was exchanged; no property needs to be returned.

42   Other people do not get upset over a divorce unless there is the threat of trouble. If a woman gets a divorce because she prefers another man, this may cause jealousy and trouble. The Kung like to avoid trouble. Trouble leads to

anger. Anger leads to fighting. And fighting is dangerous. A man might get killed.

People die, too. And thus a wife is left a widow or a husband is left alone. The man is expected to remarry as soon as he can find a wife. The widow is expected to wait until one rainy season has passed. The rains of Bara are believed to "wash the death away." But if she does not wait, no one says very much.

In such a visible life as the Kung live there is not much chance for a wife to make love with another man. Every person is a skillful tracker. Every person knows the footprint of everyone in the band and in other bands for miles around. The desert leaves trails that reveal exactly who went where and what they did. Adultery is very difficult to hide. It is strongly condemned. It can lead to trouble.

Once in a while a special arrangement is made. Two men may agree to trade wives. But the wives must agree also. This is a temporary arrangement made between close friends. Nobody else bothers about it.

And thus, if marriage comes along at the usual time and the birth of children follows, the cycle of life for a Kung man is usually divided into three parts.

First he does his bride service. He hunts for the family of the girl he marries. He continues to hunt for them until she has given birth to three children.

Second, he returns to his parents' band. Or he goes elsewhere if he prefers, for it is his choice. He continues to hunt as his children grow. His daughters marry and strong young hunters come to live with his family in bride service.

The third part occurs about the time that his daughters leave with their husbands and families. His sons return with their wives and again he has help with the hunting and can enjoy the companionship of his grandchildren.

Thus a Kung father may find that he has become head of a large family. His children have grown to be strong and patient hunters and gatherers. His grandchildren come to him for comfort and caresses and play and the loud smacking of a kiss.

43

Yet his property has not increased one bit. He still can carry all of his belongings in one or two *sacks* slung on a stick. He gains his pride and his prestige from giving things away, not from keeping them.

Squatting nearly naked by his fire, such an old, wrinkled Kung grandfather is a figure of great respect and dignity.

CHAPTER SIX

The dance of the eland

For her first six years Naoka had been pampered and nursed and carried and coddled. She had never been without love and affection. At the age of six she was still pampered and carried and coddled. But she stopped nursing.

Naoka's mother was having another baby. But it was the other children who stopped Naoka from nursing at her mother's breast. They started teasing her. Suddenly Naoka realized that she was a big girl. She stopped.

But she still cuddled up close to her mother for warmth and hugs. Her father still kissed her noisily in a way that made her giggle. Her father would smack his lips loudly when he held her on his lap. She would laugh and smack him back, imitating the sound.

Naoka had been close to her mother or her father or one of her mother's parents for all of her six years. Always someone was nearby. Always someone would carry her when she was tired, help her get food out of the fire, or pat her with affection.

Naoka had been eating hard food like meat and roots and nuts for years. She continued to nurse simply because her mother had never stopped her. Kung women do not wean their babies; they just help them to eat hard food by chewing some into a paste and plopping it into the baby's mouth.

Gradually a baby learns to like harder food and gradually it nurses less and less at its mother's breasts.

In a Bushman camp where five or six families lived closely together and every child was treated with fondness, it was easy and pleasant to grow up slowly. A child like Naoka did what she could when she was ready. Never was she pushed beyond her strength or beyond her years.

She learned how to be a woman by living close to her mother. She learned to pick berries, to dig roots, to gather nuts, to clean the food, and to prepare the meals for cooking. She learned to tend the fire, to sweep ashes over the coals so that they would not die out. She learned to sit on the right side of the fire. Naoka learned all these things in the easiest and most natural way in the world. She imitated and she helped. When she was tired, she just quit. Shama said nothing in criticism.

Just a few things were denied her. Naoka's mother taught her to stay out of the fire lest she get burned. And her mother insisted that she stay close to the camp when playing. Not many animals attack man, but lions and leopards and hyenas get hungry and have been known to pick up a straying child. And the green mamba, long as a whip and deadly with poison, respects no one who steps on him.

As a baby Naoka had loops of white shell beads tied to her frizzly black hair. She wore loops of white shell beads around her neck where they contrasted with her yellow-brown skin. The beads were gifts from Old Naoka, her father's mother. Old Naoka had spent hour upon hour drilling holes in the pieces of ostrich egg shell and then more hours grinding the shells into small circles before she strung them into loops. After days and days of this patient grinding and drilling, she hung the beads upon little Naoka.

When Naoka became eight, she was made prettier yet. With the sharp point of a *knife,* her mother scratched delicate lines on the little girl's thighs and calves. When the blood oozed, the mother rubbed charcoal into the wounds. The

cuts healed leaving black scars that everyone thought were beautiful. Each year her parents added a few more beauty marks, much to Naoka's pride.

She played with other girls. She danced and she sang. The girls would form a circle and sing songs and toss a melon to one another to indicate whose turn it was to sing.

And as she grew up, she learned that two great events would mark her life. One was the ceremony of her wedding. The other was the ceremony of her first menstruation, the ritual which would mark the time of her life when she had become a woman and had begun the monthly bleeding which indicated that she was old enough to have babies.

Naoka was married first.

Her parents had arranged her marriage to Young Toma after Naoka was born. And when Young Toma had gone through the Ceremony of the First Kill and also presented Naoka's father with an antelope, the two were married.

Naoka was ten years old. She scarcely remembered her wedding day. It was just another ceremony, only she was the chief actress. Her life did not change, for she was still a child living near home. Not until she had become a woman would she sleep with Young Toma as his wife.

In the meantime Naoka usually shared the hut with her grandmother, Old Naoka, or with Old Gisa, the other wife of Old Geishay. The grandmother's hut was ten feet from Naoka's mother's hut, and the only difference was that Naoka spent more time digging with the women than she did playing with the other girls.

Four years passed. Naoka became taller and stronger. She regularly did a woman's work, gathering and cooking and preparing food. She learned the skills needed to run a household.

And for four years Young Toma had lived with Naoka's
band, though not in Naoka's hut. For four years he had been performing bride service for Namshi, the father of Naoka. He had helped in hunting.

Then Naoka became a woman. She had squatted behind a bush to urinate when she noticed it. Mixed with the yellow urine was the red blood her mother had told her might come soon. Naoka shouted for her mother.

Immediately Shama and her grandmother, Old Naoka, ran to her with a kaross for her to sit on so that she would not touch the ground. Then they built a special hut. This *hut* looked like other huts, except that it would be used only once for the Ceremony of First Menstruation. When it was built, the two women carried Naoka into it so that her feet would not touch the ground. They sat her upon one kaross. They covered her head with another kaross so that the sun could not touch her. For five days they guarded the girl from harm. For five days of great power and danger, Old Naoka and Shama took care of the girl, feeding her, and carrying her out to the tall grass when she needed to relieve herself. Her feet never touched the ground. Had they done so, Naoka would have become thin and perhaps have died.

Old Naoka warned all the men to stay away. She warned them not even to look at the girl, for her condition was believed to be one of great magical power. It could spoil a man's ability at hunting. It would make a man more easily seen by animals. For the men, Naoka was dangerous for these five days.

And during each of the five days, all of the women danced the Dance of the Eland. They invited two old men who were not related to Naoka to join in the dance. The old men tied *sticks* to their heads to look like the horns of the eland. The women, who normally are very modest, took off all their clothing, even the aprons which they wear between their legs. Each wore only a few beads swinging from her waist.

On each of the five days they danced the Dance of the Eland. It was good magic. It was done to help Naoka be strong and healthy and to bear strong children. Nobody but the dancers watched the dance. All the other men and boys went far away from the camp, for the danger and the magic were great.

49

When the bleeding stopped, the Ceremony of First Menstruation ended. Her mother and her grandmother washed Naoka and painted red lines on her face.

But before Naoka could eat, the Choa Ceremony must be done. Each type of food was choaed.

The first time Naoka drank water, or ate berries, or ate roots, the food was treated. Old Naoka did this. She took a special root with magic power, and scraped a bit of the root into the water to choa it. Then the girl drank. Or Old Naoka held the girl's hand and the two of them picked up food together. Then Old Naoka chewed up some of the magic root and blew her breath on the food to choa it. By doing this, Naoka avoided becoming sick from food after her ceremony.

A month later when her bleeding period began again, no great notice was taken. There was no ceremony. Yet Naoka had been warned not to do certain things. She must not touch a bow or an arrow. Her touch, during her periods of menstruation, would spoil an arrow for hunting. She was not to have intercourse with her husband, because that, too, would spoil his hunting. And she must not talk to a man about her monthly periods, because even the talk would spoil his hunting.

Naoka was fourteen. Young Toma, her husband, was now nineteen.

When the Ceremony of First Menstruation was over, Naoka built her own hut. She and Young Toma moved in to sleep together. It was four years after their wedding.

And the next morning Naoka took her ironwood digging stick and her kaross and again joined the women in their daily search for food. Now she was a woman as well as a wife.

CHAPTER SEVEN

The hunt

Young Toma squatted beside the evening fire of Slender Tekay. His face was glum.

"Five days we hunted. Five days, and not a single arrow did we shoot."

Tekay grunted in agreement. He poked at the fire absentmindedly with a stick, remembering where he had placed his tsi bean to roast.

"Five days you hunted."

"And in those five days we saw only one kudu trail that looked fresh."

"Only one fresh trail?"

"Only one."

A third man joined them. Old Geishay, the father of Nai and Gao and Namshi. Geishay, the best arrow maker in the band. Geishay, who had once been a great hunter.

"Gao tells me that you hunted five days."

"But tomorrow we hunt again." It was Young Toma who spoke. "Gao wants only to rest and then we go again."

In the morning Old Geishay called Gao to him. Shortly Toma and Tekay joined them, as did three older men and two boys not yet hunters. Geishay spread his kaross on the ground and examined his five *oracle discs*. They were circles of leather, the size of the palm of his hand.

"Which one is the hyena, Grandfather?" one of the boys asked.

Geishay smiled at him. "None of them is a hyena." Then he pulled out one disc with a tuft of black hair on it.

"But this one is the lion that eats all our meat. This is the bad one."

"And what are the others, Grandfather?"

Geishay spread them on the kaross. "This is the lion, this black one. These two large ones are kudu bulls. The two smaller ones are kudu cows."

Gao spoke up. "Let us see on which side the good hunting lies."

"Ay, let us see on which side the good hunting lies."

Geishay gathered up his five discs. He shook them in his loosely cupped hands and flipped them down on the kaross in a sweeping gesture. All heads bent forward to study them. Two women standing back, leaned forward expectantly. This was man's work, but it meant meat for all hungry bellies.

Geishay spoke first to tell what the oracle discs meant. "Far to the sunrise side are the kudus. The lion has killed one of the cows. The lion is close to one of the bulls. You must get to the bull before the lion kills it, too."

Gao disagreed. "Look where they landed. They are farther south than the sunrise."

Tekay supported Geishay. Young Toma said nothing. The older men talked. Then the decision was reached. The three would hunt to the east. Geishay gave Gao an arrow. "Take this arrow, my son, and kill a kudu."

Each man gathered his bow and his spear and his quiver holding arrows, firesticks, and hollow sipstick. They all carried dried meat. Young Toma and Tekay carried an ostrich egg shell of water each in a hunting bag.

The three men walked across the dry desert. For hours they followed the dry river bed toward the horizon where the sun rose in the summer. Now, in the cold of winter, the sun rose farther to the north. On either side of them, perhaps two miles away, were the reddish sand dunes where the trees of the mongongo nuts grew.

About noon Gao stopped. All three squatted together in the shade of a bush. Since they had seen no tracks, Gao proposed that they cross the dune to the south of them and follow down that valley.

53

Wordlessly, the three men agreed.

As they passed through the mongongo nut forest, Gao abruptly led them far to the right. Once he stopped, took some fragrant brown powder from a pouch, blew it downwind, and then walked on. Tekay muttered to Toma, "Over there is the grave of his father's father."

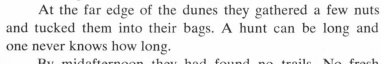

At the far edge of the dunes they gathered a few nuts and tucked them into their bags. A hunt can be long and one never knows how long.

By midafternoon they had found no trails. No fresh tracks of any animal had been seen. The only live animal was a *ratel,* the little fierce honey badger who robs the honey trees. Tekay wanted to shoot, but Gao restrained him.

"No, let us mark that spot. See that tree where he is going? That is a honey tree. We can go there later for honey."

At night they made a tiny fire and huddled over it for warmth. The men lay down so close to the fire that a gust of wind stirred ashes on them. Toma plucked a live coal from the fire and rolled it between his calloused hands to warm them. Then he held his warm hands to his face.

In the morning of the second day they came to a waterhole where they hoped to refill their shells. The hole was dry. Gao scowled at it. Tekay picked up a stick. "Let's dig a sipwell for water."

Tekay and Toma dug a hole in the dry sand. Three feet down the sand was moist. Deeper it was wet. Gao, in the meantime, had taken his sipstick and a handful of grass. Tekay scooped out a basin in the sand, packed the grass in a sort of nest to filter out the sand and waited for the water to seep in. Then he thrust the hollow reed into the grass and sucked. The first few mouthfuls he drank. Then he transferred each mouthful to an empty shell, letting the water drain down the reed which he poked into the hole in the shell.

It was slow work. The water seeped into the grass-filled hollow slowly. And it took many mouthfuls to fill one shell.

When Tekay had filled one shell, Toma took his place squatting in the hole they had dug. Then Gao drank.

While one man sucked water, the others rested and chewed dried meat. Gao told them of a hunt, years before, when he had tracked a wounded *wildebeest* three days to the east, far from the territory of his band. It was so far that when he found his game it had already been killed by three strange Bushmen. Luckily, said Gao, one of them was the son of a man named Gao, so he was accepted as a relative. He shared the meat with them, taking home only as much as he could carry.

"But do you know how they hunted?" Gao's eyes were wide with the wonder of it. "They used dogs. They taught dogs to chase the antelopes for them until the men could spear them. One man had three dogs that. . . ."

Suddenly Gao stopped. Silently he stood up, staring. The others rose quietly.

Far to the east an animal moved. Then another and another. Long straight horns. Black markings on the legs. Three *gemsboks*. Toma looked at Gao inquiringly.

Gao stooped to pinch some dust. He spilled it slowly in the faint breeze. The wind blew straight toward the gemsboks. Their scent would go ahead of them and warn the animals.

"We must circle far to the south. There, along that dry wash, then past those bushes, and come at them from the other side. Then they will not wind us."

Silently the three men walked on, crouching to keep as far out of sight as possible. When there was open ground, they crawled from one clump of bushes to the next. They took no chances. Life depended upon this hunt. Their own lives and the lives of the women and children in the camp.

Silently the men advanced. Silently the sun beat down upon them. Silently the gemsboks grazed, raising a head now and then to scan the countryside suspiciously. Once all three tossed their long horns in alarm and Gao feared for a moment that they would run away.

The men came closer. Then Gao saw another shallow dry wash that would bring them closer than ever to the game. In a silent gesture to Tekay, he pointed with his lips. Tekay and Toma followed, drifting like noiseless shadows.

Ten minutes later they were almost within arrow range. Gao carefully selected the poisoned arrow that Geishay had given him. Old Geishay, his father, the best arrow maker in the band, balanced his arrows so they would fly straight and true. Tekay and Toma selected arrows, notched them, and then the three men moved forward again.

Gao silently prayed to Gauwa, the God of the West.

The last half hour was the hardest. On their bellies against the yellow sand, with extra hunting gear left behind them in the wash, the men crawled quietly. Behind the shelter of a bush, Gao to the right, Tekay to the left, Toma waiting, the two men slowly rose to a knee, took aim at the nearest animal. When Tekay heard the twang of Gao's bowstring, he released his. This was Gao's hunt; Gao had first seen the gemsboks; Gao had the first shot.

A third twang and Toma's arrow caught the gemsbok on his first jump. In panic the three animals ran. Soon they were out of sight, running north.

The three men ran forward. Spots of blood marked the trail. Deep hoof marks, splayed out from running, marked the speed.

Quietly the three men squatted around the tracks. They studied the hoof prints, noting the size and the shape and the tiny nick on the left rear hoof. They would never forget that particular animal's track. Quietly they discussed the probable length of the chase ahead of them. Was the animal badly wounded? Deeply wounded? How long would the poison take? He had three arrows in him. Gao was sure that his had entered deep in the shoulder. Tekay's was in the rump. They disagreed on Toma's, but thought that it was high on the back.

They returned to the wash, picked up their spears and food supplies, and trotted off to trail the wounded running animal. One by one they found three arrow shafts on the trail, fallen from the arrow heads.

The sun was past noon when they glimpsed the antelopes again.

Five animals were now in the herd. But the keen eyes of the trained trackers easily picked out the trail of the wounded buck. A yelp from Gao speeded them all. A splash of red blood and yellow urine marked the trail. Eagerly they squatted around the stained sand.

From his quiver Gao took another poisoned arrow and stabbed in the bloody sand. Now the buck would surely die, for he could no longer urinate to get rid of his poison. The men stood up and followed the trail.

They camped by the trail that night, making a tiny fire and chewing dried meat and sucking a bit of water.

Before first sun they were up. In a few moments they were moving. After all this work they did not want a lion to steal their prize. And the oracle discs had foretold that the lion had taken one cow and would try to take another animal. But a dying animal is prey to any lion, leopard, hyena, or vulture that comes upon it.

On they trotted through the sand. The sun hammered on their heads; the sweat ran down their dirty bodies and left the yellow-brown skin showing through the dirt. Occasionally they stopped to drink a little water; even that was running low. Water gave life. Sun gave death.

The life-giving water and the death-giving sun were the two things most on their mind. But all they could see were the tracks of the wounded gemsbok with its nicked hoof. Here it had lain down. Here it had staggered. Here it spilled some more blood.

It was Toma, the youngest, who saw the vultures first.

"Ssst! Gao, look!" He pointed into the blue, cloudless, burning sky. Four *vultures* were wheeling slowly in the air, their wings motionless. Beneath them some animal lay dying.

Gao, tired but tough, quickened his trot. The three men, barefoot, almost naked, trotted through the thorn bushes, through the burning yellow sands, toward the dying animal that meant life for them.

The wounded gemsbok, his black-striped sides heaving, had backed into a thorn bush to face two lions. The lions prowled about and waited. They did not like the horns and they could afford to wait.

And then Gao came. He did not hesitate. He tossed a pebble at the large male lion. He spoke respectfully to it.

"We are sorry, Master Lion, but that is our meat."

He tossed another pebble and advanced slowly and with determination.

"We beg to disturb you, Great Lion, but my father's arrow is in that gemsbok. He belongs to me."

Again he tossed a pebble. Tekay tossed several pebbles. Toma sent a shower of them. The lions paused uncertainly and backed up with tails lashing slowly.

"My family is hungry, Master Lion. They need the meat of the gemsbok which I have shot with the arrow of Geishay, my father. You really must go."

At the next shower of pebbles the lions turned and walked away with dignity.

Now Gao faced the gemsbok, not yet dead, his keen horns still a menace. The three men spread, circling the animal. Gao balanced his *spear*. Then he stopped and stripped to his loincloth, leaving everything but his spear behind him. Tekay and Toma did the same.

The buck faced them defiantly, his breath gasping. Gao gave a gesture to Tekay, who knew what to do. He brandished his spear and shouted. The buck turned his neck and head, exposing the whole side to Gao. Gao lunged forward and threw the spear with all his strength. It sank into the chest of the buck. The head and the great horns jerked toward Gao. Tekay threw his spear. It stuck in the belly, blood oozing, then pouring, out of the wound. Toma, coming up beside Gao, threw, missed, and had to run around to recover his spear while Tekay laughed at him. The second time, Toma's spear went in hard, hard in the chest, between the ribs.

In ten minutes the buck was down. Warily the three men approached. The buck struggled to his front feet, blood pouring from his wounds, his eyes mad with fright and pain. Tekay seized the end of one spear and pushed it sideways, cutting the lungs on the inside.

The dying animal struggled. The men worked the spears around in circles, cutting the insides. With a gush of blood from its mouth, the buck collapsed, dead. The job of skinning could begin.

The meat would be cut and the blood saved in the stomach and the whole animal carried back to camp except for the gall bladder and the hooves.

They had walked east and south for two sleeps and run north as far as two sleeps. The trip to the camp was a little longer than two sleeps. Without hesitation, the three men knew exactly the direction to walk in, carrying their great burdens of meat, wrapped in the hide.

When the women of the camp caught sight of the hunters returning with their bloody burden, they started a song. They sang a song of triumph and praise.

The hunters had returned. All of the camp would share the meat. The arrow of Geishay had killed almost as his oracle discs had foretold.

CHAPTER EIGHT

The powers of the newly born

When Naoka was married, the boys sang at her wedding. When she went through the Ceremony of First Menstruation, the women of the camp danced. But when she gave birth to a child, she was alone.

The Kung women deliver their own babies without help. Alone the new mother leaves camp. Alone she prepares a pillow of grass. Alone she gives birth. It is the custom to do all this without fuss, without crying, without showing pain. She may bite a stick or weep silent tears, but she is not to cry out. Alone in the bush, far from the friendly firelight, surrounded by the fears of lions and the fears of snakes and mostly of the fears of the spirits of the dead, she utters no cry.

The Kung believe that birth is surrounded by power. Two great magical powers are unloosed at this time but the woman is able to control only one of them.

The first magical power comes from blood left on the ground and the bloody afterbirth. This the woman must cover with branches and grass and stones and *mark* the spot lest a hunter tread on it. Should he come too near, he would lose his power to hunt. No game would come near him. Part of his man-power would be gone.

She does not bury the blood. She simply covers it. Burying it would destroy part of her woman-power. It would be her last baby; never again could she bear any children.

When she has marked the spot to prevent evil from coming to others, the mother will return to her hut with the pink baby tucked into her kaross. She will get water from an ostrich egg shell and wash the baby and herself. And then she will nurse the baby.

Kung babies are pink when born and their skin slowly turns yellowish as they grow older. Although their hair is coiled in tight little spirals, far kinkier than any Negro's hair, they are not true Negroes. They seem to be similar to the Mongoloid people far to the east in Asia. Their wide cheekbones and their triangular faces look Mongoloid. And on the base of the spine, just above her baby's pink and fat little bottom, the mother can see a bluish spot, the same spot that is found on most of the babies born to the Mongoloid peoples of the world.

The young Kung mother does not know any of these things. Her world is bounded by the desert and the sky, by the trek from waterhole to waterhole, by the cycle of wet and dry seasons, by the knowledge that babies are born, children grow big, and people grow old and die. And when they die they become the spirits of the dead and are taken around the horizon to a house by the sunrise to be servants of the Great God, the god known as Gaona.

The young mother nurses her baby in love and pride and contentment. She has born a child to the strong hunter who is her husband. And when her husband comes and touches this first-born baby with love and pride, he will give the child a name. He will call it by a name he has known all his life. If it is a boy, he will name it after his own father. And if it is a girl, he will name it after his own mother. It is the custom.

The other great magical power that comes at birth is something the mother cannot control at all. This power has to do with rain and the changes in the weather. It is a great power and a mysterious one. The Kung call it Entlow. It gets into a human being at the time of birth.

Some babies get a good Entlow; theirs can bring rain which is life giving. The rest get a bad Entlow which can bring the cold dry winds of winter, the terrible hunger of Gaw. Mothers often guess what their baby's Entlow is by observing the weather immediately after the birth. But the action of Entlow is tricky and one cannot always be sure.

The power of Entlow can be shown by burning part of the body, usually a few pieces of hair or some urine, in a fire. Burning these from a person with good Entlow will bring warm rain, giving life to the people. Or if there has been too much rain, it might be stopped by burning the hair or the urine of a person with bad Entlow.

Despite the Kung's knowledge of how Entlow works, they never seem to do much about it. The Kung perform no ceremony to make it rain even though they are dying of thirst. And no one has ever reported seeing them burn hair or urine to control the weather. They believe it can be done, but apparently they do little with this belief.

The Kung partly understand heredity. They believe that both father and mother contribute to the makeup of the baby. They think that the baby is made from the semen of the father and from the menstrual blood of the mother. And they are aware that children do resemble their parents in their looks.

But Entlow is not inherited. It does not come from either the father or the mother. It just comes.

Entlow affects the weather in many mysterious forms. Its force is very complicated because the Kung believe that certain animals also have it. Big animals with hooves have Entlow. They are the gemsbok and the hartebeest, the eland and the kudu, and the stately, giant *giraffe*.

Now if a hunter with one type of Entlow kills an animal with a different type of Entlow, then the weather will be affected. The Kung have observed that hunters have killed a kudu and that shortly afterward it rained. Obviously something in the interaction between the two Entlows caused the rain. It is difficult to explain all this, especially to those of us who have never seen Entlow work and do not understand just how it works. But the Kung have seen it work and they believe it.

The Kung do not perform any ceremony to control the rain. They do have a Rain Dance. But it is performed at the time when the rains usually start and is used to celebrate the coming of the rains, not to cause their coming. That is quite a different thing. The Rain Dance drives away evil. It does not bring rain.

Thus, when Naoka, feeling the rhythmic straining of the muscles of her womb, slipped away from the flickering firelight to the darkness of the bush, she felt face to face with great and unseen powers. Her baby could change the weather. Her baby might bring life or death to others. Her baby's Entlow, by interacting with the Entlow of some kudu killed on a far-off sand dune, might bring the searing drought that can kill those who live in the desert. Or the two Entlows, interacting, might bring the life-giving rains of Bara and turn the yellow desert to green. Naoka could not know.

But she knew that a baby had been growing within her. She knew that her husband had helped to form that baby. She knew that a baby might follow their sleeping so closely together as they had done ever since the Dance of the Eland. She knew that a baby might come when he had snuggled up close behind her in loving warmth. And she knew when he had fondled and caressed her until she would accept him in mating, that in time she might have a baby.

She knew when the baby had begun, for the monthly bleeding from her vagina which a year earlier had marked her coming of age as a woman had stopped. And this stopping of her monthly bleeding marked her arrival at a new stage in life. In eight moons more, the older women told her, she would have her baby.

For nine moons the union of the sperm from Young Toma and the egg from Naoka had grown and grown. Naoka's body had changed to accommodate this new life.

Naoka knew little of the complex changes going on within her except that her bleeding had stopped and that slowly her belly bulged out in front. She did not know of the sheltering womb which grew larger as the baby grew. She did not know of the muscles surrounding the womb which grew stronger but were held relaxed until needed to squeeze out the baby. She did not know of all the miracles within her to shield the tiny life from outside harm. She did not know of the placenta which separated the blood of mother and child. She did not know that her baby was growing inside a water-filled sack to cushion it from bumps.

Naoka did not know that when the nine moons had passed the adrenal glands of the fully grown baby sent a chemical message through the blood stream to the muscles of her womb. The message told the muscles to contract. And the slight pains began. The pains were something that Naoka did know about.

When she felt that rhythmic straining, Naoka left camp alone. She felt pain and love and joy and fear.

Out of sight of the camp she crept behind some bushes. She scooped a hollow in the sand. She laid bunches of grass for a pillow. Then she knelt above the grass with her knees spread wide on either side of the hollow.

The contractions came faster now. She pressed with both hands on the bulge of her belly. She felt a sudden bursting as a rush of water poured out of her vagina. Again the rhythm of the muscle squeezings speeded up. She braced herself, clinging to a branch.

The baby was coming out head first. It hung there for a moment while Naoka clung to a bush, half dizzy. The muscles of her womb squeezed once more. The weight of the baby helped. And a tiny infant dropped to the grass pillow. It had come out of the same opening of Naoka's body that Toma had entered nine months earlier with his penis. Relief and joy and love surged through Naoka's mind.

With the sharp edge of a stick of wood, she cut the umbilical cord. Its job was done. No longer would the blood

65

vessels carry food to the baby. Now the baby must eat and breathe on its own.

But the activity inside her was not over. Soon she felt something more coming out, and she moved her baby so that the bloody pulp would not fall on it. Naoka did not know that this afterbirth was part of the miracle of protection provided by her body to shield her baby from infection. She did not know that the placenta had allowed her blood to carry food and oxygen to her baby's blood without actually mixing the two blood streams. She did not know that the wastes from her baby's body had been carried to the placenta and there transferred to her own blood. But she did know that this afterbirth was something she must hide from the men in her camp. She must conceal it lest one of them step too close to its magic power and lose his power to hunt.

Quickly Naoka covered it with grass and with branches. When she felt strong enough, she picked up her baby and walked back to camp. But before she left, she marked the spot by breaking off some branches and twisting a bundle of grass into the fork of a branch. The hunters would see this sign and would walk far around to avoid it.

Clutching her baby to her, Naoka walked slowly back to camp. Without a word she took an ostrich egg shell filled with water and washed her baby clean. Then she washed the red stains from her thighs. She did this quietly, but inside her heart was singing.

She wrapped her baby in a soft skin and nursed it at her breast.

Young Toma had been talking by another fire. He tried to appear casual and not to show too great concern. However, soon he came over to his young wife and squatted beside her. She unwrapped the skin to show the new father his son, and Toma poked one finger delicately at the tiny fist. Toma and Naoka smiled together.

"We shall call him Baby Kwee," Young Toma said. And Naoka smiled in agreement. A first-born boy should be named after his father's father.

Toma planned a hunt for the next day. The chief responsibility of a father is to feed his family with meat. And suddenly Toma felt the pride of fatherhood.

Birth is not always pleasant or easy. Sometimes a woman has trouble and must call upon other women for help. Sometimes a woman has a baby nursing still, and the new baby is following too closely upon the last. A woman must work to gather food, and she must carry her nursing baby with her strapped to her side or her back. Digging roots and gathering melons and hauling firewood is hard work. With a baby it is harder.

But with two babies it is impossible. No mother can nurse two babies and carry two babies and do the work that a Kung woman must do. She may survive through the warm wet season when food is easy to get, but when winter comes followed by the dry and bitter winds of Gaw, the three will not survive. They cannot survive. All three will weaken and die.

The Kung have known this for many, many years. They know that it is better that two live than that three die. And if the extra baby must die, it is better that it die quickly.

Alone a young mother must decide this. If she still has a baby nursing when she slips into the bushes, she knows what she must do. She digs the shallow basin in the sand, but this time she makes no soft pillow of grass. In reality she has dug a shallow grave.

It is not easy to kill one's baby. The only way that a mother can do it is to keep telling herself that it is better that two will live.

Quickly then, before the newborn can utter a cry, it is dropped into the grave and covered with sand and smothered. Quickly, before her firm resolve has been softened by mother love.

CHAPTER NINE

How do you talk to them?

As do other peoples, the Kung marry and have children. Having children creates new families. Marriage links two families together. And all the people in these families have special ties, special bonds. We call them relatives or kin. Just think of all the names we have for people in our families: husband, wife, daughter, son, brother, sister, uncle, aunt, grandmother, grandson, brother-in-law, and many more.

The Kung recognize many relatives and have names for their kin. Some of the relatives they name are the same as ours. Some are quite different.

Here are some Kung names for relatives:

Father	*ba*
Mother	*dai*
Son	*ha*
Daughter	*kai*
Husband	*hoa*
Wife	*tsoa*

But notice how differently the Kung name brothers and sisters:

Elder brother	*go*
Elder sister	*kwi*
Younger brother	*tsee*
Younger sister	*tsee*

The Kung think it is more important to say whether a child is younger or older than to state whether it is a brother or a sister.

Our word *cousin,* for example, doesn't make it plain whether our cousin is a boy or a girl. Nor does it tell whether our cousin is younger or older. Nor on our father's side or our mother's. Nor the child of our parents' brother or sister. Nor whether our cousin is a first cousin, a second cousin, or a third cousin. Nor whether our cousin is once-removed, twice-removed, or three-times-removed. We lump a lot of different relatives under that one word *cousin.* Over sixty different kinds of relatives we call "cousins."

The Kung lump all boy cousins under the one word *goona.* They call girl cousins "toon."

When we speak of a grandfather we might mean our father's father or our mother's father. We lump the two together in the same word. The Kung lump both grandfathers under the word *goona*—yes, the same word used for boy cousins.

And both grandmothers are lumped under the word *toon.*

Now don't think that the Kung cannot tell the difference between a boy cousin and a grandfather. They can. And you can tell your father's father from your mother's father. If there might be confusion, you add his name. So do the Kung.

A Kung boy will call his boy cousin "goona." And that cousin will call him "goona." Our word *cousin* is reciprocal. It works in either direction. So is *goona* a reciprocal term. An old man calls his grandson "goona," the grandson calls his grandfather "goona" also.

If you realize that we lump different kin under one word, you can more easily understand that the Kung do it too. Only they lump differently. They make distinctions that we don't. And they ignore distinctions that we think are important.

For another example, we call both our father's brother and our mother's brother "uncle." The Kung lump them just as we do. They go a little further and make their word reciprocal. A boy calls his uncle "tsoo." A man calls his nephew "tsoo."

The practical result of having kin terms is that you know how to act toward people. You give them gifts or you do not. You joke with them or you do not. Kin terms usually include the people that you wouldn't think of marrying.

So far the Kung system sounds easy. In some ways it is even simpler than our system of naming relatives. But the Kung, although their weapons, their tools, and their houses are simple, do not have a simple system of kinship. They make it complicated in several ways.

One way is that the Kung name a child after a grandparent. Young Toma was named after his father's father, Old Toma. His sister, Young Khuana, was named after their father's mother, Old Khuana. And Toma, in turn, will name his first-born son Kwee, after Tall Kwee. The second son is named after the mother's father. The second daughter after the mother's mother. Each name skips a generation. A child is named after a grandparent, never after a parent. One result of this Kung practice is that few names are used. The Kung have forty-six names for boys and forty-one for girls.

The second way of complicating the naming of relatives is the Kung's use of nicknames. And these change. Young Toma becomes Lazy Toma if he is not a good hunter. Toma Feet has big feet. Toma Belly Button has one that sticks out. Lame Toma walks with crutches. Toma Beard has some hair on his chin.

A third way is with namesakes. Suppose you were a Kung named Toma. Anytime you were to meet your namesake, that is a person with the same name as your own, you

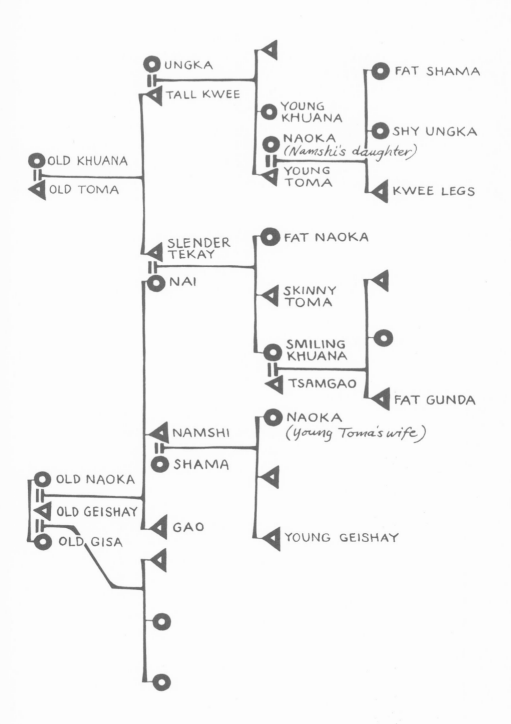

would feel related to him. More than that, you would know how to act toward him. And if a visitor had the same name as one of your relatives, you would treat him as you would a relative, calling him by a special name.

For example, if you were to meet a visitor named Kwee, your father's name, you would call him "tsoo," the term for uncle.

If the visitor had the same name as your mother, Ungka, you would call her "tlika," the term for aunt.

If the visitor had the same name as your sister, Khuana, you would call her "kwi." If she were younger than you, you would use "tsee."

If the visitor had the same name as a brother, you would call him "go" or "tsee," depending on his age.

And if the visitor was called Toma, do you know what you would call him? You would use the same term that you use for grandfather, for cousin, and for grandchild. You would call him "goona."

The Kung believe that persons with the same name must be descended from some common ancestor way back. So they treat them as relatives.

The fourth way of complicating the naming of relatives is by calling in-laws by special names. Almost every in-law that you could think of is called either "goona" or "toon." Do they sound familiar?

And the fifth way of complicating the system of relatives is that the men use one set of terms and the women use another set. Those we have used here were only the terms used by men. When a woman speaks, many of the words are different.

The value of knowing a kin term is that you know how to act toward a certain person. For example, the Kung do a lot of joking and teasing. Some of their jokes get pretty rough. But you are expected to take it all in good humor and not get angry.

The important thing to learn is with whom you make

joke. Kung children learn very young. And they first learn with whom you may never, never joke.

Brothers can joke with brothers; sisters can joke with sisters. But a brother and a sister may not joke with one another.

Children may not joke with parents, nor parents with children. Children may not joke with people of the same generation as their parents. One does not joke with uncles or aunts, nor with nephews or nieces.

A Kung may joke with anyone that he calls "goona" or "toon," and that includes a lot of grandparents, cousins, and grandchildren. And he may joke with a lot of in-laws.

A man may tease his brother's wife. "What a big, fat, lazy thing you are. The hyenas would drag you away if you were not so fat."

She can tease him back. Joking and teasing always work both ways. Joking is reciprocal. She may remark that he is unworthy of ever getting a wife. Or that if he does get a woman, she will run away with the first real man who comes along.

One man may tell another that he could hunt better if he did not spend so much time sleeping with his wife. And the other may respond that the first man has such an enormous penis that he ought to marry an elephant wife.

The Kung say that this sort of teasing and joking teaches people to hold their tempers. And holding tempers is important when you must live closely with others and depend on their help.

But joking and the kin system do something else that is very important. The whole system lets people know with whom they may marry. Usually a man and a woman who may joke also may marry. Those who cannot joke may not marry. Brothers and sisters may not joke. Nor can they marry. Parents and children may not. Uncles and nieces, aunts and nephews may not. But cousins may not marry even though they may joke.

Marrying a close relative is called incest and is forbidden. The Kung's way of naming relatives stops anyone from committing incest. Marriage and joking go together. Taboos on joking and taboos on incest go together.

Thus, when Kung visit each other's camps during the summer, they always know how to behave with the new persons they meet. Everyone fits into the system, somehow.

CHAPTER TEN

Preparing the poison

Men work hard at hunting. But it is irregular work, a surge of great effort followed by several days of resting and talking. In between hunts men have other work to do. Their life is not all work, and only for a few months of the year, during the bitter time of Gaw, does keeping alive become difficult. Most of the rest of the year living is relatively easy.

Women, on the other hand, work at digging roots almost every day. Yet roots are not exciting and many of them do not taste very good. The roots and berries and melons and nuts which the women bring home are the bulk of the Bushmen's diet. Women feed the camp daily. Men provide the occasional banquets.

Hunting takes preparation. Arrows must be made, bows carved, bowstrings twisted, egg shells pierced, poison prepared, skins cured, karosses made, bags made, strings for snares twisted. Men also find time to visit and to talk, plenty of time.

Men make the digging sticks. They select a tough branch of ironwood and peel the bark, then shape one end flat and sharp. Women use these more than men do, but almost everyone carries a digging stick. And in an emergency it can be used for other purposes, such as clubbing a small animal that one has caught or even hitting another person if

75

you are angry. But Bushmen control their tempers and try never to show their anger. It leads to fighting.

When a large animal has been killed, the men usually save the whole skin. It serves temporarily as a basket to hold the blood and the water from the animal's stomach and this the men need to drink when they are far away on a hunt. Later the skin will serve as a kaross or cape for someone. But if no one needs a kaross, the skin can be eaten. It is pounded to powder in a wooden *mortar* with a wooden *pestle* and then eaten. Those who eat powdered skin say that it is delicious.

Frequently the hide is cured into a kaross. For curing a skin the Bushmen use urine which they collect by asking the family to urinate into empty tsama melon rinds. When enough is collected, the workman soaks the skin in the urine and works it with his hands until it is soft. He also may use several plants to help the curing process. The urine softens the skin and the folding and working and rubbing make it soak all the way through. When dry, the skin remains soft.

Or the hide can be used to make a small carrying bag. Sometimes the men take the cured skin of a small animal such as a duiker and turn it inside out to make a bag. They tie the legs together and tie the neck for the bottom of the carrying bag.

In the winter, when both antelopes and men stay close to the waterholes, men snare small animals like the steenbok. To snare an animal one must first have a strong cord. The Bushmen make the cord out of a fibrous plant. They split the plant's leaves and pull out the long threads which they soften in water and then twist into string. A man might roll the fibers on his thigh to twist them into string. He would hold the finished end with his toes, pulling it away from his thigh as he rolled. And he would continually add new fibers so that the string will not pull apart at any one place. String is valuable only if it is strong. From such a string a man can fashion belts for a loin cloth or a woman's apron, and nets for carrying, as well as snares.

Setting snares requires preparation. First the men in

the winter camp agree where each will set his line of snares. Once a man has his area, he studies the tracks of the little steenbok which he hopes to snare. Then he builds a fence. He drags dead bushes in between live bushes until he has closed off most of the passageways the animals might use. He thus forces the steenbok to use one of the openings left in his fence.

In these openings he sets a *snare*. Right where one of the animals might step, he drives several pegs in a circle. He loops a noose around this circle of pegs and ties the end to the top of a small tree bent over so it will spring back. To hold the noose ready, he arranges a trigger of sticks set in tiny notches in the pegs. The steenbok's foot kicks the trigger out of the notch. The bent tree snaps upright, pulls the noose tight round the steenbok's leg, and the animal is held with one foot high in the air, thrashing about to escape.

If the knots are well tied and the rope does not break, the steenbok will be alive when the hunter makes his daily rounds. The hunter will kill it with a club, reset the snare, and hope for another kill. A hunter might get one steenbok a week which would give him a dozen pounds of meat.

Sometimes, of course, the hunter arrives too late. The steenbok has been eaten by a leopard or a hyena. Snarelines must be visited regularly. And they are made only in winter when both animals and hunters stay close to the waterholes.

Another tool the men use in hunting looks like a long fishing pole. It is a flexible branch with a sharp hook on the end. When a hunter locates the burrow of a hare or some other small animal, he pokes and probes the hole with this stick. When he has pierced the animal and feels it struggling, he pulls it out. Small game like this is eaten by the one who gets it; it need not be shared the way large game is shared according to custom and good manners.

Water carriers are made by men, also. When they find an ostrich nest, they may kill the ostrich and take both the ostrich and the eggs, but often they just frighten the bird away and take some of the eggs.

Then they peck a hole carefully on one side of the egg.

The shells are thick and strong. The hole must be small so that it can be plugged with grass or leaves when carrying water. But first the yolk and the white are taken out for eating. The men pound the shell on the sand, mixing up the yolk and the white so that they will come out of a small hole more easily.

The most important hunting tools are the men's bows and arrows. Men do many things. They make many things. But they think of themselves as hunters. Not till a boy has proven himself a successful hunter is he called a man. Not till he has become a hunter can he marry. And his first gift to his bride's parents is the gift of an antelope which he has killed. To be a man means to be a hunter.

Men take pride in their bows and arrows and their spears. They make them with care. They mark them as their own. They give arrows to other men, for the owner of the arrow which kills an animal gets some of the meat. Arrows are given and given and given again. Like most of the weapons and tools the Bushmen make, arrows are continually passed from hand to hand. The giving of gifts is important.

A Kung *arrow* is usually made in three parts: the metal point, the wooden main shaft, and the bone link that fastens the two together. The sharp point was formerly made of bone, softened and whittled to shape. But today, the point is made of iron wire taken from a fence or gotten in trade from a white farmer or a Bantu trader on the edge of the Kalahari. A Kung arrow maker takes a five-inch piece of iron wire and pounds it into shape with a rock hammer on a stone anvil. Even if he heats the wire in his campfire the pounding is hard work and takes time. He shapes one end into a small triangular point. Then he sharpens the edges by rubbing them on a stone. The other end of the wire, about three inches long, is left for a shank.

This wire shank fits into the hollow link bone. Although the link bone fits tightly enough to hold the arrow together, it is meant to pull off and fall free when the animal is hit, leaving only the arrow point in the animal. For the metal point carries poison on its shank. And it is the poison which does the killing.

The other end of the link bone fits into the hollow reed of the main shaft. Some arrow makers use a short piece of wood fitting the bone link to the main reed shaft. This main shaft must be straight. The whole arrow must be straight. It has no feathers to guide it or to twist it in flight. It is straight and balanced and poisoned. A well-made arrow may well mean the difference between a lunch of tasteless roots or a banquet of kudu steak.

The small arrows of the Kung do not fly far, perhaps thirty or forty yards. They carry little wallop. It is the poison that kills, weakening the animal until the Bushman hunter, running behind, can finish the job with his spear.

Sometimes the careful arrow maker will wrap the iron wire shank with animal sinews. He will moisten the sinew in his mouth till it is soft enough to stretch. Then he wraps it tightly around the shank, tying the ends. As the sinew dries, it shrinks and hardens. The poison will stick to the sinew better than to the iron.

The poison clots the blood and causes some paralysis. The animal gasps and struggles for breath. No antidote for the poison is known, so the Bushmen are very careful with it.

The poison is also one reason the Bushmen show good manners toward each other. An angry man might shoot a poisoned arrow.

When a hunter has made several arrows and wants to prepare the poison, he takes a number of precautions. Usually he works away from camp where no tiny child will come near. He works downwind so that no poison will blow into the camp. Later he burns all the poison that is left over.

The poison comes from the pupa of a certain beetle that lives in the Kalahari Desert. The larva, when it is grown, crawls into the ground to form its pupa. There it begins its change into an adult beetle. While it is underground and while it is in the pupa stage it is poisonous.

80

Somehow the Bushmen discovered this. They dig up the pupas which they know can be found underneath a certain type of bush. They collect these carefully, wrapping and tucking them away safely inside a bag. Then they make their arrows and prepare to apply the poison.

The hunter builds a tiny fire and works on an old rag of skin that he can throw away later. He must be sure there are no cracks in the skin of his fingers. He breaks open a pupa and pulls out the wriggling grub with a straw. He taps the grub to mix its insides like a woman puddling the pulp of a tsama melon, only more gently. Then he breaks off the head and squeezes the deadly body fluids onto the arrow.

The insides come out like toothpaste and are spread along the wire shank of the arrowhead, but not on the point nor on the sharp edges. The sharpness might too easily scratch someone and kill him accidentally, but a good shot at an animal will bury the arrow deeply enough so that the deadly part will reach its blood.

The arrow maker smears the *poison* on. Then he takes out another pupa and repeats the process, twisting off the head and smearing that poison on. When the shank is covered, he lets the poison dry near the fire. Then he applies another layer, using up eight or ten grubs on each arrow.

The poison remains deadly for years, though it may dry and flake off the head in a year's time. When finished, the hunter will wipe all his arrows carefully, dropping any sticks that have touched poison into the fire. Then he burns the skin. Then he washes his hands. The poisoned arrow, when dry, will go into his quiver, point down, ready, waiting, and deadly.

CHAPTER ELEVEN

Climbing into the sky

The Kung see the world mostly in terms of male things and female things. The strong sun, which burns and kills, is male. The round full moon is female. But the new moon, showing its crescent horns, is a male. The clouds which move quietly in gray mists are females and so are the huge white cumulus clouds. But the dark black stormy clouds are males. They bring hard rains and lightning. Rains which fall gently are called female rains and those that strike destructively are males. You can tell the difference later by the footprints of the rain on the dust. Female rain leaves little dots all over, but male rain leaves a big, heavy print. The Kung will copy the rain's footprints in the sand, showing female rain with a gentle touch of the fingertips and male rain by bunching the fingers to punch a deep hole.

The male rain brings lightning. Although lightning is dangerous, you must not show fear. Instead you should stare at it to let the light of your eyes frighten it away. Then the lightning will not harm you, the Kung say.

Also, the Kung say that there are two worlds. The one we live in is the upper one. The underworld beneath us is much like ours. It, too, has deserts and animals and people. It has rivers and hills and mongongo nuts. But the two worlds are separate, although perhaps the deep waterholes which hold water all during the dry season of Gaw are tun-

82

nels down to the underworld. Some of the Kung think that the Great God of the East climbed up from the underworld which he made first. Aside from this, the Kung do not say much about the underworld.

Some of the Kung say that the stars are great hunters and the greatest is the Morning Star, who strides up the sky to his home in the east just before sunrise. Others think the stars are the eyes of dead people. They say that when a star falls it is the sign of a Bushman's death.

The falling of a star did not always mean death. Long ago when the earth was young and the sun was small and all the animals were persons, the Moon spoke to the *hare*. He gave him a message for mankind, "As the Moon dies and returns again, so shall man die and return again."

But the hare mixed up the words. When he delivered the message, he said, "Man will die and not return again."

And thus men died. When he realized that the hare had given the wrong message, the Moon got very angry and cursed the hare and crashed his fist into the hare's face. "You, too, shall die." And his fist split the hare's lip even as it is split today.

But the hare kicked back. He scratched the Moon's face as you can see now at night.

And that, the Kung say, is why men die. If the hare had not confused the message from the Moon, men would live forever; they would grow big and small and big and small just as the moon does when it waxes to a full moon and wanes to a crescent moon.

Yet men do die. The Kung, like all other people of the world, love the members of their family. Death comes as a blow. And like other peoples of the world, they have certain practices, certain ways of behaving at death.

They bury their dead. With their digging sticks they dig a grave deep enough to bury the person in a sitting position, facing the east, where his spirit will go. He is tied in a sitting position, with legs bent, arms across the chest, and head on his knees. In a man's grave the Kung place his bow

and arrows; in a woman's, her digging stick. And as they fill in the grave with the earth, each person throws in some dirt to help the person to remember them and to help the spirit leave without bothering anybody.

Hyenas have been known to dig up bodies, so the Kung drag thorn bushes over the grave, and stones. They also destroy the hut that the dead person lived in and break most of his possessions, because nobody wants to use them. And last of all, just before they leave the campsite, never to return, they kindle a small fire near the grave. They kindle the fire beyond the grave and toward the place where the person had been born. And beyond that, in the same line, they thrust a reed into the ground as a marker.

Over the grave and the dead person's broken possessions the Kung sprinkle the powder of the sasa, a fragrant herb. And for years, as long as they can remember, whenever they pass near this spot, they will blow a little sasa toward it.

This ritual is done upwind from the grave and the corpse. For when the spirit of the dead person leaves, it travels with the wind. By sunset the spirit will have left, blowing downwind and dangerous to man.

The spirit is led by the Gauwasi, the spirits of those who died before. Up into the sky they climb, on ladders as fine as silk from a spiderweb. Then they travel far to the west to the house of the God of the West. But they do not stay there. The Gauwasi conduct the spirit in a circuit of the southern sky ending up at the huge house of the God of the East.

Near the house of the God of the East, the Great God with seven names, stands a huge tree. On the tree the Gauwasi hang the spirit of the dead man. The Great God then kindles a fire under the tree to make a smoke which floats upward to the spirit hanging on the tree. The smoke converts the spirit into a Gauwasi.

Once the spirit has become a Gauwasi, he also becomes a servant of the Great God. He becomes a servant and a messenger and will travel up and down the sky and the earth for the Great God. He brings sickness and evil to men. He kills men.

The Kung fear the Gauwasi. They fear even to talk about them, since they are the source of most of the evils which befall men. But at one time they do talk to them. At the one time they talk to the gods, they curse them. That time is at the Medicine Dances.

The Gauwasi do not remember their former family. They do not take revenge for old injuries. They do evil because they are ordered by the Great God, not because they are angry with men.

But occasionally the Gauwasi do kill people for their own reasons. The Gauwasi take husbands and wives in the sky world, but up there, just as on earth, people tire of husbands and wives. And if a Gauwasi wants a new wife, he may look about for some beautiful young Kung girl and kill her to come up to the sky to be his wife. Or a female Gauwasi may select a strong and handsome young hunter to be her husband.

Some of the Gauwasi are full of mischief. They make scary noises at night just to frighten people. Or they will steal up on a hunter who is stalking an antelope and pinch him or frighten the game.

The chief business of the Gauwasi is to kill men. This is done at the orders of the Great God, but the methods are left up to the Gauwasi. They might have a person struck by lightning, or gored by a wounded buffalo, or mauled by a lion, or even bitten by a mamba, the deadly poisonous snake of the desert. In whatever way men die, the Gauwasi make it happen.

They also make men die slowly, by sickness. They carry tiny little bows and arrows to shoot sickness into people. It takes a good Medicine Dance to cure such sickness, but it can be done. A strong medicine dancer can curse the Gauwasi and force them to remove the sickness.

All of this world was created by the Great God. All of the sky and the desert, the sun, the stars, the moon, the animals with Entlow, the ordinary animals, the Gauwasi, and the human beings. All of them were created by the Great God. And he taught man how to make arrows and bows, spears, digging sticks, and how to dance and sing and hunt.

The Great God created himself long ago. He also gave himself seven names and all of them the Kung fear to pronounce out loud. The Great God knows that he is the ultimate power. "I go my own way. I do the things that I please. No one can command me."

The Great God also created the Lesser God who lives at the sunset. Then he created a wife for each of them. And when he tires of his own wife, he swaps wives with the Lesser God for awhile. Men may swap wives, too, but first they must ask their wives if it is agreeable.

The two gods have children. Their children are much like the Gauwasi but they are friendlier. They often help men who are in trouble. And they listen to men's prayers quite readily.

The Lesser God of the West is called by the same names as the Great God of the East. One name of the Great God is Big Gao, and this is a name the Kung may use in everyday talk. The other names would make the Great God angry. If he heard them being spoken, he would come to see who was calling him, regardless of what he was doing. And then he would be angry.

That is why the Kung do not speak the seven names. And that is why they are not written here.

What does Big Gao look like?

Nobody has ever seen him, but they think that he is large. Some think he rides a huge horse across the sky. He carries a spear and a gun.

The Lesser God has been seen by the Kung.

Some of the medicine men, during their trances, have seen the Lesser God. More than that, they have talked with him. Some have cursed him and shrieked at him. But they do not agree on what he looks like. Some think he looks like a mouse, others like a tiny man with sand-colored hair. One medicine-dance curer, after seeing the Lesser God in a trance, said he saw a small yellow man who was very fat. Another man described what he saw as more like a *wart hog*. And one curer, bearing the burden of sickness from a patient and hurling it back at the gods, saw only a small misty, gray cloud.

Curiously enough, there is a third being that the Kung know about. This third being seems to resemble the two Gods, Big Gao of the East and the Lesser God of the West. He goes by a number of names and he seems to be the hero of a number of Bushman stories about the Gods. Some Bushmen call him Pishiboro; others call him Tukwee; some call him Mantis after the insect. The Kung Bushmen call him Gaona or Old Gao which is exactly the same name as the one they use for the Great God of the East. Only this Old Gao is a rascal full of tricks. He is a creature who does terrible wrongs. And he is also a great hero. When the Kung whisper the name Old Gao, they mean the Great God. When they shout the name and laugh and giggle, they mean the hero and the rascal.

The Kung talk easily about Old Gao and they tell many stories about him.

CHAPTER TWELVE

When the earth was young and the sun was small

As he lies near the warmth of his campfire, a Bushman grandfather sometimes tells stories about Old Gao to his grandchildren. In some of the stories Old Gao seems to be the first Bushman. In others he appears to be the first God, who creates things. Sometimes he is foolish, at other times very clever. Sometimes he is generous and helping, at other times greedy and cruel. Perhaps he reflects how people behave.

Several Bushman tribes tell such stories. The Kung of the Kalahari tell these stories.

OLD GAO TALES

Long ago when the world was young and the sun was small, nobody knew how to cook meat because nobody had any fire. But one day Old Gao visited his brother-in-law, the ostrich, and ate a tasty meal of cooked meat. He had never eaten cooked meat before and he wanted to see how it was done.

At the end of his visit, Old Gao only pretended to leave. He circled around his brother-in-law's home and hid in the bushes. He saw the ostrich bring home some meat, and then take two sticks out from under his armpit. One stick he lay on the ground, the other he twirled rapidly on top of it until he had made fire. Then he cooked the meat.

Later Old Gao came on another visit. This time he said he wanted to play *janee,* the game of throwing the nut and feather tied with a long string high in the air. Janee takes a lot of running and one must be fast to catch the janee before it hits the ground. Each time Old Gao kept throwing the janee farther and farther, making the ostrich scramble to catch it. Finally the ostrich had to flap his wings. And when he flapped his wings, he dropped his firesticks.

Quick as a mamba, Old Gao seized the sticks and broke them into little pieces and threw them all over the world. Now all men have firesticks, and all men make fire and cook their meat. Thanks to Old Gao.

*   *   *   *   *

Long ago when the world was young and the sun was small, Old Gao had two wives who were sisters. The wives had a brother who was an ostrich, a very fat ostrich. Old Gao was terribly hungry one day and he was hungry for fat. He wanted fat. When he saw the folds of fat hanging on his brother-in-law, the ostrich, he got hungrier than ever.

Now, Old Gao was tricky and he wanted that fat. He walked up to the ostrich and said, "Do you know that the sweet plums are ripe on the plum tree now, down by the waterhole?"

"Let's go eat some," said the ostrich, greedily.

When they got to the tree, Old Gao kept pointing out ripe plums and riper plums. Always he pointed to plums that were higher and higher up the tree. Finally the ostrich was standing on his toes and flapping his wings to keep his balance as he stretched for the plums. As he flapped his wings, he revealed the great lumps of fat under them. Old Gao had his knife ready. He grabbed a chunk of fat, sliced it off with his knife, and ran away to eat it. The ostrich cursed him. "May all your bones be broken. May you die in agony."

Old Gao just laughed and stuffed his mouth with fat.

*   *   *   *   *

Another time Old Gao was really hungry. This time he wanted to eat all of his brother-in-law, the ostrich. He set a snare, tying the cord to a strong young tree bent over. Then he tricked the ostrich into running into the snare. The snare caught the ostrich's feet, jerked him up into the air and killed him.

Old Gao cut up the meat into chunks and cooked them in his big *pot*. But he ate too much. He got a terrible case of diarrhea; his bowels were so loose that he made a mess all over. When Old Gao's wives came home, they suspected something was wrong, especially when they saw the terrible mess Old Gao had made, and smelled all that meat cooking in the pot.

Just then the waterpot boiled over and the steam made a great explosion. It threw chunks of ostrich meat in every direction. The chunks of meat gathered themselves together and became an ostrich again, and the brother-in-law ran far away where it was safe. Far away from Old Gao.

*   *   *   *   *

Long ago nobody knew that males and females were different. Nobody knew how babies were born. This was when the world was young and the sun was small.

Old Gao had been pulling so many tricks on his wives that they resolved to get even with him.

They dug a deep hole and then they defecated in it. They filled the hole half full with their manure. Then they called Old Gao to come see the baby antelope who had fallen into the hole.

When Old Gao came running over, full of curiosity, and leaned over the pit to see, they shoved him in. They shoved him right into the hole they had dug and then half filled with their excrement.

Poor Old Gao. He slithered around like a wet snake in a swamp trying to get out of that mess. His wives howled and howled with laughter. But when they saw him finally climb out and go to the waterhole to clean himself up, they climbed a tree to hide.

Then Old Gao saw them up there and for the first time he noticed their sex organs. Suddenly he realized what they were for. He pulled his wives down out of the tree and had intercourse with them right then. And that was how Old Gao got so many children.

*   *   *   *   *

Old Gao was always after women. He liked to make love to women and he was not particular whose woman it was. When Old Gao's son married a beautiful wife, Old Gao wanted her for himself.

First he changed himself into an antelope fawn with big soft eyes, hoping that the wife would take the fawn for a pet. But the wife wanted to eat the fawn instead, so Old Gao ran away.

Old Gao kept trying to go with the women as they gathered the roots and berries. The next time he changed himself to look like his own sister. Then he followed along with the son's wife and slept next to her and raped her at night while she slept. The wife knew that something was wrong when she woke up in the morning. The other women suspected it was Old Gao up to his tricks again. But they decided not to say anything to their husbands for fear they would kill Old Gao.

Once Old Gao, who was very generous, was out hunting with his sons. They killed a large eland, skinned the animal, cut up the meat, and began to carry it home.

On the way they met a man who asked them for a share of the meat because he was hungry. Old Gao gave him a large piece.

The man walked away, hid the piece of meat in a tree, ran ahead on the side of the trail, and again asked Old Gao for some meat. Old Gao did not recognize him and gave him more meat. The man hid the meat, ran ahead, and for a third time asked Old Gao for some meat. The sons warned Old Gao not to give any more to this trickster, but Old Gao thought the man was hungry. He gave him another large piece.

A fourth time this happened. On the fifth time, Old Gao gave away his last piece of meat and returned to camp empty-handed. He had no meat for his two wives.

Desperate, not wishing to appear to be a poor hunter, he picked up a stick and beat himself on his own buttocks. He knocked himself inside out. Then he cut some of his own insides up for meat and brought it home to his wives.

They cooked the meat but then complained that it was too tough to eat. They threw it away. Poor Old Gao!

*   *   *   *   *

Old Gao's son took the form of a mantis, an insect, about two inches long, that seizes other insects and eats them. His forelegs are folded in a way to make him look as though he is praying, and so he is often called a praying mantis.

Mantis married an elephant wife, but the two fought a great deal. Finally Mantis took a quill from the porcupine and killed his elephant wife. Then he began to eat her. But her blood ran down the hill and across the plain and far across the desert to the hut of her elephant father.

The father smelled the blood and knew right away what had happened. In anger he called all the other elephants to

93

his aid. Thousands came. They formed a huge army and they charged across the desert to attack little Mantis, the son of Old Gao.

But Mantis knew what to do. He flew up into the face of the first elephant and he killed him. Then he flew into the face of the second elephant and killed him, too. Each time he farted once in the face of an elephant, and the huge beast died. On and on he flew, farting in the face of each elephant until the entire desert was covered with the bodies of dead elephants.

BEGINNINGS

Stories about the beginnings of things have been told by every people under the sun. The Bushmen, who once lived all over southern Africa, as we know by the hundreds of rock paintings they left, told these stories. They are about the Sun or the Moon, how the animals became as they are, why the Bushmen live in the desert, why people get married, and why men must die.

Most of these stories came from a collection of Bushman tales made one hundred years ago. A white man named Bleek studied the Bushman language and wrote down many tales told him by a convict, a tiny Bushman named Dream.

Dream had been driven off his hunting lands by a white farmer. Then he was arrested for killing an antelope on those same lands. For this crime a white judge sentenced Dream to hard labor at hauling rocks.

The Kung no longer tell these stories. Perhaps they have forgotten them.

      *   *   *   *   *

Long ago when the earth was young and the sun was small, there was a deep hole in the earth. This hole was so deep that it had no bottom, no bottom at all. When you dropped a rock in that hole, you could never hear it hit bottom.

Everybody lived in that hole at first. All the men, all the animals lived in that hole. No one died. Soon it became so

crowded that they quarreled over the space. At last the men drove out the animals.

Once they were out and began eating the food on the outside, the animals wandered off. The antelope went to the rivers for grass. The lions went after the antelope. They all wandered away.

The men stayed behind. But then they began quarreling. At last they drove each other out.

The hole is still there. Go and see for yourself.

*   *   *   *   *

When the earth was young, the Sun was very small and lived on the earth along with the Bushmen. The Sun had light and heat shining out from his armpits. Wherever the Sun lay on the ground there was light and heat. But the rest of the earth was cold and dark.

Many of the Bushmen were cold. They wanted heat and they wanted light. They would rather have the Sun up in the sky so that they could see to hunt.

Finally one woman told her sons what to do. She told them carefully, "Wait for the Sun to lie down and sleep. When the Sun is sleeping, you must creep up to him softly and quietly. Then pick him up gently and throw him high into the sky."

The Bushman children obeyed their mother. Gently they approached the Sun as he lay sleeping. Gently they lifted the sleeping Sun. All together they tossed him high into the sky. They could feel the heat from the armpits of the Sun as they lifted him. They could feel the heat as they tossed him. As the Sun went up, the children cried out, "Stay up there, Sun. Stay up there and shine upon us. You must stay in the sky and shine upon all of us."

And that is how the Bushman children threw the Sun 96 up into the sky. Now the whole earth has light and heat from the Sun.

*   *   *   *   *

The Sun stays in the sky and lights the earth. Day after day the Sun moves about the sky and chases away the darkness and the Moon. Every day the Sun chases the Moon. The Moon likes the night. The Sun prefers the day. Every day the Sun chases the Moon. When he gets close enough, the Sun stabs the Moon with his knife. Then the Moon dies slowly until nothing is left but his backbone. The Sun leaves the Moon's backbone and gradually the Moon grows big and fat again. Then the Sun chases him again and stabs him once more with his knife. Again the Moon dies slowly until nothing is left but his backbone. Gradually the Moon's backbone grows full again and he becomes a big Moon. The Sun chases him again.

*　　*　　*　　*　　*

Long ago the Bushmen did not die. They lived forever. Not until the Moon sent the Hare with the message to people did death come. But you already know that story.

*　　*　　*　　*　　*

Long ago when the earth was young and the sun was small, the animals were like people. They talked and quarreled among themselves. The Ostrich was the chief because of the noise he could make with his wings. Even the Lion feared the Ostrich.

The Lion and the Ostrich were friends. They hunted together. The Ostrich would chase the antelope toward the Lion and shout, "Kill one for me, Lion, because I have no teeth."

The Lion would kill the antelope and let the Ostrich choose his meat first, because the Ostrich was the chief.

The Ostrich picked out all the soft inside parts. He ate them and went to sleep. The Lion ate the rest. One day he looked at the Ostrich sleeping and snoring with his mouth open. Then the Lion laughed, for the Ostrich really did not have any teeth.

97

From that day on the Lion no longer feared the Ostrich. That is how the Lion became the chief of all the animals.

*   *   *   *   *

Long ago when the earth was young and the sun was small and the first Bushmen lived on the earth, the men used to live in caves and hunt animals. But the women lived in grass huts and ate mongongo nuts and berries.

The men and the women did not even visit each other. They had nothing to do with each other.

One day the men became careless. While they were hunting ostriches, they let their fire burn out. When they returned, they had no fire to cook their meat.

Five men lived in the cave at that time. One of the men was sent down to the river to borrow some fire from the women.

The man found a woman gathering nuts and seeds. He asked her for some fire so that he could cook his meat. She told him to come to her hut to get the fire.

Then she noticed that he was hungry. She invited him to eat. She ground up the seeds and roasted them and fed the man. He liked the taste of the food. He liked it so much that he decided to stay for another meal. He never went back to the cave.

Back in the cave, the four men were getting very hungry. Finally they sent a second man to get fire from the women. This man also met a woman who fed him at her hut. He liked the food so much that he decided to stay. He forgot all about the other men in the cave.

Back in the cave, the three men were very, very hungry. At last they sent out another man to get fire. This man also found a woman who invited him to her hut for a meal. She fed him good food. He stayed with her. He forgot all about his friends in the cave who needed the fire.

The last two men became desperate. They were starving. The meat was spoiling. They decided that one of them had to bring back fire. The fourth man left. He found a woman and asked her for fire. She agreed but invited him to eat first, and made him forget all about returning.

The last man was angry, despairing, and starving. His meat was spoiled in front of him. He gathered up his weapons, his bow, and his arrows, and fled far away looking for game to hunt.

And that is how the first Bushmen learned about marriage.

                *   *   *   *   *

Long ago when the earth was young and the sun was small, the Bushmen and the Bantu Negroes lived together. In their village was a large piece of rope. Half of it was strong leather rope. The other half was weaker, made of twisted fiber. The leather was made from the skins of cattle. The fiber was made from the wild plants of the desert. The two ropes were tied together in a knot.

One day a Bantu said, "I shall use this rope." And he picked up the leather end of the rope.

At the same moment a Bushman said, "I shall use this rope." And he picked up the fiber end.

The Bantu and the Bushmen quarreled. Then other Bantu came and grabbed the leather rope to pull it away. The Bushmen all grabbed the fiber rope to pull it away. They had a huge tug of war, shouting and yelling at each other.

Suddenly the knot broke. The Bantu, pulling hard on the leather rope, stumbled backward. Rolling and rolling, they tumbled far away into the river country where the grass grows green and the cattle grow fat. Here the Bantu became herders of cattle and tillers of gardens.

But the poor Bushmen fell in the other direction. Still clinging to their fiber rope, they tumbled far into the dry and

99

dusty desert. To this day they live there, hunting and gathering.

      Some of the old Bushmen say, "If ever we have another tug of war we must be sure to grab the leather end of the rope."

*   *   *   *   *

All of these things happened long, long ago when the earth was young and the sun was small.

CHAPTER THIRTEEN

The fears beyond the firelight

When the cold winter winds begin to warm with the approach of summer, the Kung Bushmen struggle through their hungriest months, the hot and dry season of Gaw. For the hot sun comes to the desert long before the wet rains. The hot sun dries up the remaining waterholes. As they disappear, so does the game.

Gaw is the time that the Kung fear. In very bad years, Gaw is the time when mothers who have been foolish enough to keep two babies must kill one of them mercifully or else die with them both. During a very dry Gaw, old parents, blind, or helpless, or unable to hunt or to gather their own food, may be left to the hyenas as the starving band straggles away in a desperate search for water. In those rare years only the strong can eat; no man can provide enough food and water for a useless mouth. Old men and women fear the three moons of Gaw, when the cruel sun burns down through the lifeless trees and sucks the moisture out of every living animal.

The Kung do what they can to survive. They imitate the desert snakes, the tortoises, and the *lizards* which hide under

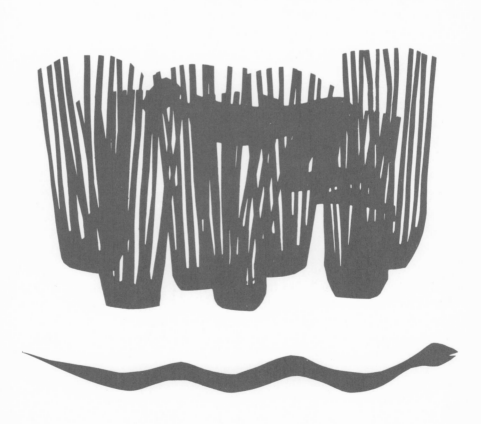

the rocks by day or bury themselves in the sand. The Bushmen will scoop out shallow pits and cover themselves with sand, knowing that the deeper layers of sand are cooler than the upper. The sand will keep them from losing too much water in sweat. It may keep them from dying. In truly desperate times, they may line the pits with leaves and bark, urinate on them, and lie down on the moist leaves, hoping in this way to save a little moisture in their dried-out, wrinkled skins.

The desert plants, after ages of adaptation, have grown roots that store water during the wet moons for nourishment during the dry. The Bushmen have learned to recognize these plants, and can recognize the withered vine, thin as a thread, that marks where a huge, water-bulged root lies deep underground. The Bushmen, as do all men, use nature's tricks to man's advantage. They dig up the roots and squeeze out the water to survive the moons of Gaw.

But it is a bleak and bitter time, the worst of the year.

The Kung fear other things, too. On any day the Gauwasi, climbing down from the sky on tiny threads, may strike with sickness. The Gauwasi may turn a lion into an attacker just because of Big Gao's whim. Hunters who often have driven lions away from a wounded eland may suddenly find one day that the lion will turn to bite and claw.

The very ground is dangerous. For lying in the grass, hidden and deadly, lies the green mamba with a poison more deadly than that of a Bushman arrow. Strong hunters have been killed or crippled for life by the fangs of the *mamba*.

And all around the desert lie enemies, the strangers, the people who are not the Kung. The Kung see them. These enemies are men, big men. They are the big black Bantu-speaking Negroes and the big red-faced Europeans with guns. Whatever their color, the Kung fear them, for the Kung are small, and the black herders and the white farmers raid the Bushman camps, killing the old people and stealing the children to bring them up as slaves and servants. Such acts are illegal, of course, but in the wild bush country there are few policemen. All the Kung can do is hide. They have two names for those strangers: they call them "the dangerous persons" or "the hoofless animals," for they are as dangerous as the lion who has no hooves.

Yet the desert is the Bushmen's home. The Kalahari, which scourges them with heat and thorns and drought and hunger, also protects them. The heat and thorns and drought and hunger keep out the slave raiders and the child stealers. The land of the little Kung Bushmen is the land that the big men did not want.

Many fears drive the Bushmen into the security of their families. Only there can they find the friendliness and the security and the love and affection which human beings need in a dangerous world, a world that is indifferent to man.

But the family and the band which offer so much protection can also threaten. Living as they do in isolated little clusters, the Kung sometimes become jealous. They gossip about each other. Then anger grows like a cancer. A man grows jealous of the way his wife looks at another man. Tempers grow short during the heat. And all men carry poisoned arrows.

Fear of nameless things surrounds the Kung. When a man sits in his hut, he always sits on the left side as he faces out; his wife sits on the right. If he ever sat where a woman had been sitting, he would lose his ability to hunt. Some mysterious power, left in the ground by the woman's sex organs would enter his body and defeat him. As for the woman, if she ever sat where a man had been sitting, she would catch a disease that would cripple her children.

It is such fears that make the women mark the spot where their menstrual blood is spilt, so a man will not come near it. Men are warned not to look at a girl during the
Ceremony of First Menstruation; the risk is too much.

And they fear to utter the names of the gods. "That is a death thing," they say, lowering the voice to a whisper and looking about fearfully. Older folk fear less, for they know their time is almost used up.

Older folk can speak the names of the gods with less fear. An old man can even talk about things which were taboo when he was young, such as the names of the sex organs of an animal that he is skinning. It is two old men who dance the Eland Dance with the women. They imitate the courtship of the eland bulls. Old men fear the spirits less. They have seen too many others die. They can accept the future more calmly.

And if it must happen in some dry and hungry winter, an old couple can watch the rest of the band leave them. They can watch the starving men and women, with strings knotted tight around their aching bellies, break camp and leave them behind. They can face the day of the *hyena* with dignity.

CHAPTER FOURTEEN

Giver of the arrow

Most of the time the hyena is kept far away. Most of the time the Kung eat reasonably well and get along reasonably well. It is the rare year that is so wretched that old couples are abandoned.

No, the problems of the Kung are much more ordinary. They must learn to live with the everyday fears that beset them—the fear of anger or jealousy, or the fear of the many nameless forms of death and disease that Big Gao can send by one of his invisible messengers, the spirits of the dead.

The Kung have worked out some fair ways of living with their fears. They know all their relatives, and they recognize as relatives everyone who has a name the same as their own, or the same as their father's, or their mother's. This brings a lot of additional people inside the circle of love and security and sharing.

Sharing seems to be the key. They give gifts to each other frequently. An old woman may spend day after day grinding ostrich egg shell beads to make a long string of beautiful white beads. And when she has finished, she will give the beads away, draping them about the neck of a niece or a grandchild. Later on, of course, that person will return a gift. If a year passes and no gift is returned, the old lady may hint or even ask directly for something.

Men who are skilled arrow makers make arrows for other men. When an arrow brings down a buck, the Giver of the Arrow always gets a large chunk of meat that he in turn may share.

Accumulating possessions would make other men jealous. And one would simply have more to carry to a new camp. It is much easier to give a tool to someone and then borrow it back when you need it. Certain objects are needed by every man: arrows, a bow, a knife, dance rattles. Each woman needs a digging stick and a kaross and ostrich egg shells. But axes or musical instruments, bowls, spoons, a janee toy, *pipes,* sasa powder, or red powder, these things can be borrowed. It is not necessary for each person or even each family to carry objects which can be borrowed or made.

Everybody knows who owns things. If you wish to peg an eland skin out on the ground and scrape it clean, it is easy enough to whittle wooden pegs. And you can get enough other folk to help you. Each man brings his knife.

Sometimes a man will actually have too much. If he does not wish to give it away, he may store it in a tree, ramming it in a crotch. A hide which has not yet been cured might be kept this way. A year or so later the man may come back and finish curing it. And if he had a few other things he did not wish to carry and no one else wished to carry, he might roll them up in the skin. A year later they would be there still, unless some animal had chewed on them. No Kung would take them. No Kung would steal anything.

Jealousy of others is kept down by the sharing around of wealth. The more skillful can make more things and give more things. They derive a certain prestige from giving. In this way the leader is often the poorest, having given away most of his possessions.

Yet in the end it all comes back. The tools and weapons and toys and beads move slowly in visible currents from owner to owner. And each person remembers and knows. Sometimes a gift does not go to the person who expected it; his feelings are hurt. A substitute gift must be made.

It all comes back in another way, too. It comes back in good feeling. The giver feels better than the receiver. And the Giver of the Arrow gets meat as well as prestige.

When it comes to the sharing of meat, the Kung have definite customs. They kill and eat most of the large animals in the Kalahari except the meat-eating animals which are all tabooed. The meat eaters are the lion, leopard, jackal, hyena, and wild dog. And they never eat monkeys because they consider them close kin to man.

The animals they hunt are the wart hog, ostrich, eland, kudu, giraffe, antelope, gemsbok, wildebeest, hartebeest, duiker, steenbok, the hare, and the springhare.

However, an individual may avoid some animal because a medicine man has told him not to eat it. Thus one man may never eat *porcupine* or fox. The medicine men, themselves, may occasionally eat an animal that all others avoid, the skunk, for example. And as one gets quite old, the taboos on food are often lifted. Old women can eat almost anything, even lions and jackals. That may make up for the fact that when they were young, before their Ceremony of First Menstruation, they were not allowed to eat the springhare or the steenbok.

Sharing is important to the Kung. When a group of hunters has made a kill, they cut the animal up and bring it to camp and share it in certain customary ways. In the heat of the desert, the meat would soon spoil. It must be eaten now. And it is. In a few days, the entire animal is gone, and almost everyone in camp has eaten the same amount. Then when another group of hunters makes a kill later on, they share their meat also and thus the first hunters are repaid. On it goes. Some sharing occurs because of obligations to kin, some by obligations of bride service, some by obligations to the Giver of the Arrow, some by obligations from having received a gift during the last hunt.

Butchering an animal takes skill. The Kung hunter learns when he is young how to separate the skin most easily from the flesh. He learns how to roll the antelope on its back

and to slit the throat and the belly and down the inside of each leg, and then to cut out the stomach and the rumen and use them for holding the blood. The rumen is the first stomach in grazing animals and is often filled with undigested grass and the water from the grass.

The blood is saved and carried to camp. So is all that the Kung consider eatable. And they eat most of the animal, tossing away the gall bladder, the testicles, and the hooves, but not much else.

If several hunters killed a large animal, they would share it. Not all animals are shared; the small hares and foxes and rabbits are considered too small to share. The man whose arrow first hits a large animal owns the meat. He keeps a big share for himself, reserves a big share for the Giver of the Arrow, and divides the rest between the other hunters.

The hunters carry the meat back to camp, hauling it on their shoulders or on carrying sticks. Often blood is running down their bodies as they proudly bear the meat in. The women, seeing them from afar, will shout and start a song of welcome. It is a proud occasion.

Then comes the second sharing. Each hunter then cuts up his meat and gives some to his wife and some to his parents or some to his wife's parents, depending on which family he lives with. He also may include brothers and sisters or brothers-in-law and sisters-in-law.

Later that same day a third sharing takes place. All those who got big chunks give some to others. An old arrow maker, too feeble and too blind to hunt, will proudly cut up half a hindquarter and share it about, deriving great pleasure and prestige in giving. He is living again the glorious days of his proud youth when he was a great hunter.

Should anyone be missed, he is taken care of in the last sharing when the meat is cooked. No one is left out. No one in camp would sit and eat meat while another person, ten feet away at another fire, had none. That would be a disgrace.

Giving and sharing hold the Kung together. Giving and sharing tie men to each other in mutual obligations and prevent the jealousy and envy of unequal wealth. Although one might envy another man's skill, that envy is lessened when one eats a meal gained by the other's skill. And envy of another's skill also encourages the other men to get out and hunt, as is the duty of men.

Good manners hold in the eating of meat, also. Each person may cook and eat his own, but he soon learns to cut it up to save some. He may hang strips on a bush to dry into a tough and chewable piece of dried food. But he will not stuff himself sick as Old Gao did in the story of his greediness.

The Kung talk a lot. They talk out their anger and their jealousies. They let it be known when they feel slighted. They sing songs which tell how badly someone once behaved and in this indirect way, let the children know how people feel about such behavior. Talking, they seem to feel, is better than sulking and letting the worm of discontent grow within.

In addition to the strain of twenty to thirty people living constantly in full sight of one another, the Kung also have to live with the tensions that come from the unknown. The Kung must handle the dangers from the spirits of the dead in order to live on this earth. However the Kung do not live a good life in order to reach heaven. Instead, they live a good life in order to get along on earth.

The spirits can be dealt with in several ways.

One can pray to them. "Father, you made me and gave me the legs to hunt. Then why do you not show me where the game lies?"

Or, "Big Gao, let us have rain. Give us rain. We need rain to wet the earth and to grow the plants that we eat."

Or, "Big Gao, help us to kill an animal. Help us, for we are dying of this great hunger."

Anybody can pray. The Kung have no trained priests. They do have medicine men; in fact all men are medicine men, but some are more skillful than others. So whatever the occasion, a Kung may pray aloud or pray softly. He prays for game, for rain, for good hunting, for relief from sickness or from the grief of death.

"You took that person while we still needed him and loved him. Why did you take him when we loved him?"

"You gave me this child. Do not take him now. What will I do if you take this child?"

But the strongest way to deal with the fears of the unknown is by the Medicine Dances. Only at the Medicine Dances can a sick person be cured, can the Gauwasi be forced to take back their disease. The people who attend are not only protected; they can watch while the medicine dance curer removes the sickness from a body and hurls it back into the faces of the gods. The people dance and sing and clap. They help the curer work up to that pitch of fever which enables him to challenge the spirits. They listen to him curse the very gods themselves.

CHAPTER FIFTEEN

Take back this evil

The Great God of the East whom the Kung call Big Gao is the one who gives men sickness and death. Yet this same god also gives men the power to cure sickness and to avoid death.

Big Gao gives this power to certain men at certain times. The certain time is at the Medicine Dance. And the certain men are those men who feel particularly skilled at curing. All men can cure. All men know how to cure; but only certain men become experts. It is something that just happens: the men do not train as priests; the touch of the Great God falls upon them. The touch fell upon Namshi, brother of Nai.

*   *   *   *   *

Three women sat by a small fire singing and clapping. They were Nai, Ungka, and Naoka. Near them sat a sick girl, who was quiet. Shy Ungka was the second child of Naoka and Toma. Then more women came out of the darkness. Each one carried a burning torch. After tossing her brand upon the fire, each joined the singing group. They sat in a circle around the fire. The song carried the melody, the Song of the Gemsbok. The clapping carried the rhythm. A few of them clapped at a different beat from the rest, making complicated rhythmic patterns. Children wandered slowly over and joined them. A few boys danced.

Then, the men danced out of the darkness. They came with their ankle *rattles* of dry cocoons shushing softly. They came with their muscles tense. Several had ostrich plumes in their hair. They came out of the darkness singing and dancing and formed a larger circle around the women. The sick child watched them, her eyes intent.

The men made tiny steps, stamping hard on the accented beat, bearing the weight on one foot and stepping a quick rhythm with the other. Then a hop and a change of feet and another quick, pulsating rhythm. The men sang. The women sang. The women clapped with their fingers spread stiff.

They danced harder and harder. In the firelight, sweat gleamed on their golden bodies. Beyond the circle one could see only the darkness of the scrub and the desert. The stars gleamed high above. Dust rose ankle deep in the circle as they kept the rhythm, all of the men jumping at once and coming down hard with a thump which seemed to shake the earth. Harder and harder. Until. . . .

A scream! Namshi, his ostrich plumes white in the flickering firelight, stands rigid, steps aside from the circle of dancers and closer to the fire. His arms rise, stiff and hard, the muscles knotting, the veins standing out, his face contorted. Then slowly, like a great tree falling, he crashes over, his stiff body half in the fire.

Two men drag him from the fire. They rub his body. The dancing goes on, harder, more intense. Namshi is in the half-death. His spirit has left his body and until it comes back, he is in great danger. The women sing louder. The tempo of the clapping increases. The men dance faster; they stamp harder.

Namshi recovers partly. He stands up, flinging aside his helpers with a toss of his strong arms. With a roar he rushes through the fire, scattering the coals. He charges through the circle of women and into the darkness, screaming. He returns to the fire and dips his hands in it. He picks up hot coals to rub his sweating hands dry. He washes his face in flames.

115

Then he turns to Shy Ungka, the sick little girl who has been staring intensely at her grandfather.

Namshi bends over her. He claps his left hand on her back and his right hand on her chest. He rubs her body with his hot dry hands. He pulls the evil out. He groans with the effort as he draws out the sickness that the Gauwa have sent into her body. The evil comes into his arms. It creeps up his arms and into his chest. His hands flutter like a snared wild dove on her chest. His breath comes in gasps and moans.

Then Namshi steps to a woman sitting nearby. He touches her briefly, his hands beating like wings, hot and dry and drawing out evil. He touches another and another.

He breathes in moans, gasping, gurgling, struggling for breath against the evil, which he is drawing into his own body. When he has taken as much of the dread evil as his body can contain, he will hurl it out. With one wild shriek he will spit in the face of the gods and curse them for sending evil to mankind.

The men dance on. Faster and faster. Namshi touches all the women, all the children. He draws out all the evil and he protects them with goodness. The men dance faster. Their feet stamp the earth; they are ankle deep in dust now; the dust from their dancing clings to their sweaty bodies.

With one last scream, Namshi, the curer, leaves the fire. He rushes once more into the darkness. He screams at the gods. He calls them filthy names. "Your faces are covered with excrement. You have no shame. You walk about naked. Take back your evil!"

It is a dangerous moment. Namshi and the dancers are challenging the powers of the gods and the powers of the gods' messengers, the spirits of the dead. They are not praying; they are commanding. "Take back your evil!"

With one last shriek, the curer collapses. Several men
116 assist him, rubbing his body and blowing in his earholes. They dip their fingers in the sweat from their own armpits to anoint him. Another man collapses in a trance, and others help him, rubbing and moaning.

The dance goes on. The women sing and clap. The tempo slows to its former pace. The curers lie asleep, dragged aside from the circle. The men dance on.

All night they dance. They dance the Gemsbok Dance and they sing the songs of the Gemsbok Dance, for the gemsbok has strong power, strong magic.

Occasionally a woman will drag over some dry wood to fuel the fire. Some will leave to sleep and then return. The boys, too, are dancing and occasionally a woman or a child will join the dance, then shriek and fall over just as Namshi did.

And when dawn comes gently over the desert before the flaming sunrise the women sing the Sun Dance Song, and then, suddenly, the singing stops. The clapping stops. The dancing stops.

Weary and exhausted, they stand up and walk to their huts to sleep. Under a bush, still unconscious, Namshi will sleep till noon. He has won his dare with death. He has faced the gods and flung a challenge into their faces and protected the people from the evil of the Gauwa.

And Shy Ungka, surrounded with love and caring and goodness, feels better.

CHAPTER SIXTEEN

Rolling a new fire

When Old Toma finally died, the next headman should have been his eldest son, Slender Tekay, who had helped his blind father for years. But when Old Toma lay dying, Slender Tekay was already dead. Just two moons earlier he had been bitten by a mamba. The poison had slowly rotted away one leg before it killed him. He died in the rainy season of summer. Old Toma died that autumn.

The son of Slender Tekay was Skinny Toma. But that young hunter was far away performing his bride service. And thus, Tall Kwee, Tekay's brother, became headman.

Kwee and his wife, Ungka, had hunted and gathered over the band's territory for many years. They knew where all the food plants grew. They knew the two reliable waterholes and all of the temporary ponds. They knew where everything grew and they knew the boundaries.

Kwee became headman. A Kung headman is not a chief. He does not command. Kwee was first among equals. He inherited his position because his father had been headman and his father's father before him. Should a headman die without a son, a daughter might become headman. Women have done well at the job.

A headman does not give orders. He listens and talks and he announces a decision that everyone has quietly agreed to in advance. On questions of hunting men always listen with most respect to the strongest hunter.

Thus Kwee listened. He listened to Gao and to Namshi and to a new hunter, his strong young son, Young Toma. For Young Toma was now returned to the band with his wife, Naoka, and their three children, Kwee Legs, Shy Ungka, and Fat Shama. Young Toma had done bride service for Namshi, his father-in-law, for almost twelve years. And when Toma returned to his father's band, Namshi decided to come along, too. Toma was a strong hunter and Namshi liked meat.

The Kung bands vary in size. Namshi's band had both good hunting and good water. But it was large. And according to Bushman custom, one may leave one band and join another in which he has kin. A Bushman can join any band where he has kinship with the headman, or any band where his wife has kinship with the headman, or any band where he has a name relationship with the headman.

A headman may seem to own water and territory and the plant food. Actually he is merely the keeper. He guides the use of the food. The food belongs to the people. No one really owns the land, because you cannot eat the land.

Yet each Bushman learns the boundaries of the area under his headman. Since animals do not respect such boundaries, it is all right for a hunter to chase wounded game into the territory of another band. He may not hunt outside his territory, but he may chase a wounded animal. And, should he meet members of that other band, he would display his good manners by giving them some of his meat killed in their land.

One of Kwee's duties as headman was to announce when the camp would move. During the rainy season a band moves often from shallow pan to shallow pan. They eat the tastiest food. They visit with distant relatives. And they avoid the food by their permanent waterholes, saving it for the lean months of Goom and Gaw, the dry season of winter.

Kwee had no great trouble deciding when to move. He could hear the women grumbling about the long walks each day to find roots. He sensed when everyone was ready for the long walk to another waterhole. Then he simply announced that the next morning they would go.

Moving is easy. Huts are just abandoned, for new huts are easily built. Each woman carries her own kaross either as a garment or as a carrying bag. Each person carries his own tools and weapons. Women carry their own shells and wooden mortars and digging sticks and scraps of food. Men bundle their possessions into a skin bag and hang the bag on a stick. The bag may hold dance rattles, ostrich feathers, poison grubs, extra arrows, firesticks, extra food in the form of dried meat or nuts, a guashee for music.

After Kwee announced one cool wintry night that they would leave, the packing the next morning took only a few minutes. Then, with no ceremony, they left.

Kwee led, followed by the other hunters. Then came the children. The women followed, trailing their long karosses on the ground as they walked. The men were nearly naked, for the sun was warm.

Without hesitation Kwee headed across the desert, knowing exactly which way to walk. Behind him the band followed in single file. The next waterhole was thirty miles, one sleep, away. Since they could walk fifteen miles in a day, they would make only one stop. They would reach their next winter camp on the evening of the second night.

That first night they reached a huge baobab tree that Young Toma remembered climbing as a boy. Here Kwee rolled a fire and everyone gathered fruit. Kwee Legs climbed the wooden pegs in the huge tree. None of the women bothered to built a hut. Ungka poked two sticks into the ground to signal to her husband where the *door* of the hut would be had she built it. The sticks told them both where to sit. By such simple customs the ancient taboos are enforced. By such simple devices the ancient fears are avoided.

120

Naoka built a fire nearby, within reaching distance of Ungka's fire. She and Ungka could not speak to one another, being daughter-in-law and mother-in-law. But that bothered nobody. Ungka spoke loudly to Young Toma and Naoka listened and replied loudly to Young Toma as Ungka listened. Custom can solve many difficulties set up by custom.

Naoka's three children tumbled about playing. Shy Ungka and Fat Shama climbed on the back of their big brother Kwee Legs who was named for his father's father and for his speed.

On the second day of the long walk, Young Toma carried Shy Ungka several times. She was five years old and could walk. But Toma was proud to carry her.

On the second night Kwee reached the waterhole. He led the band up the side of a reddish sand dune past the remains of last year's camp and the fainter ruins of the camp of the year before. Kwee selected a new spot near two large trees which would provide shade and shelter and branches to hang things on. When he lifted the load from his shoulder and laid it on the ground, Ungka knew immediately where to build her hut and her fire.

Quickly she set to work. Each woman gathered branches for her hut. The children gathered mongongo nuts. Ungka selected her curved branches, dug holes in the ground, and tamped the butt ends in solidly. She laced the tops together and then gathered bunches of grass. These she twisted into shocks suitable for thatching. Neatly and efficiently she built the layers up from the bottom. Last she tied the whole house together with cords, securing it snugly against the winter winds.

Next Ungka gathered nuts, tossing them rapidly into the pocket of her kaross. When she had a meal, she picked up dry firewood and dragged it home. On her return trip she passed her last year's campsite. There, near the tumbling ruins of her old hut were her nutcrackers, the small stone resting on the large flat stone, untouched for a year. With her free left hand, she balanced these on her hip and dragged the firewood home.

How many years, she wondered, had she used those same stones? Her son, Toma, had grown and married and now had three children. Ungka could not count beyond her fingers, but she knew that it had been many years that she and Kwee had been coming to this camp. Kwee had come here as a child.

Kwee had unpacked his firesticks. With tinder and twigs ready, he began the ritual the headman always performs in a new camp. He rolled a New Fire. Twirling the stick expertly in the notch of his baseboard, he spun and spun until a curl of smoke from the dry tinder indicated that the fire would start. With the skill of long practice, Kwee dropped his firesticks and thrust the glowing tinder under some dry twigs. Soon the fire was crackling upward as Kwee fed it bigger and bigger sticks.

Then Kwee dropped in a small piece of meat.

God of the West, keep evil away from this camp.
Keep sickness away from this camp.
Keep death away from this camp.

Toma came to get the New Fire. He picked up a flaming *brand*. Namshi took one. Gao took one. The boys who were living apart from their families took one. Old Gisa, the second wife of Old Geishay and now his widow, took one. Kwee picked up the last brand and carried the New Fire to his own hut. Behind him, the New Fire slowly died. But it burned brightly in front of each hut.

The camp settled in. The babble and murmur of Kung voices filled the air. A hunt was planned.

In the hut near his father's, Young Toma sat by his wife and watched their two girls. A dream troubled him; a sudden glimpse into the future bothered him.

For as he had picked up the brand of New Fire, Young Toma suddenly realized that he might well be the next headman of his band. For years the band had been led by Old Toma who had been known as Tall Toma when he was young. If Kwee were to die now, the duties of headman would fall to him, to Young Toma.

122

And in his imagination he saw himself leading the band across the desert to a waterhole. And he saw himself, as his father and his grandfather had done, building a New Fire for a new camp.

What Old Toma had done, Young Toma would do. Only when that time came he would no longer be called Young Toma. He would be just Toma. Someday, later on, he would become Old Toma.

And that long-legged, fast-running, ten-year-old son of his, Kwee Legs, would soon make his First Kill. And he, Toma, the proud father, would scar the chest and arms and forehead of another tough and clever young Bushman hunter. Those black tattoo marks of manhood would signify that Kwee Legs could marry the girl he and Naoka had already picked out for him. A hundred miles across the desert a fat and frolicking five-year-old girl was growing up to be Young Toma's daughter-in-law.

The darkness of night closed in softly over the camp as Toma dreamed. A ripple of laughter jerked him awake. Gao was asking him about hunting. Tomorrow they would kill an eland. Everybody in camp wanted fresh meat. Tomorrow an eland.

Fat Shama nursed at her mother's breast. Naoka poked some nuts out of the coals and cracked them expertly. The endless talk and joking and laughter of a Bushman camp rippled among the campfires.

Kwee Legs and two older boys had already settled in by their own fire. A log tossed on a fire shot sparks upward toward the bright winter stars.

Gao had seen the tracks of an eland near the waterhole. Tomorrow they would hunt an eland.

For a moment the distant coughing rumble of a lion's roar hushed every living thing. Then the talk picked up. More jokes and bantering. Fat Shama slept on Naoka's breast. From the boys' fire came the rhythmic thrumming of a *bow*. A young hunter sang a sad song about the year that the melons tasted bitter.

Night had fallen on the Kalahari. Another night. Another season in the endless round of seasons of wet and dry. A new campsite in the endless round of campsites. A New Fire. New Kung hunters growing strong.

And tomorrow they would hunt another eland.

ACKNOWLEDGMENTS

Most of the information in my account of the Kung is based upon the field studies of two anthropologists, Lorna Marshall and Richard Barry Lee.

Mrs. Marshall and her family studied the Kung in that part of the Kalahari Desert around Nyae Nyae Pans in South West Africa. Her published studies appear in the journal *Africa* (1957, 1959, 1960, 1961, 1962, and 1969). She also has written a more comprehensive account of the Kung which appears as a chapter in *The Peoples of Africa* edited by J. L. Gibbs (Holt, Rinehart and Winston, 1965).

Most of Mr. Lee's studies were done about fifty to a hundred miles east of the Marshall study area. Mr. Lee worked at Dobe in that part of the Kalahari lying in Bechuanaland. His studies are reported in his doctoral thesis, *Subsistence Ecology of !Kung Bushmen* (University of California at Berkeley, 1965), available from University Microfilms, Inc., Ann Arbor.

The basic facts and interpretation of Kung society in my account are primarily those reported by Lorna Marshall and Richard Lee in the works cited above. I thank them both. However, the narrative and any errors are mine.

In addition, I have used data from Elizabeth Marshall Thomas's *The Harmless People* (Knopf, 1959) and *The Lost World of the Kalahari* and *The Heart of the Hunter* by Laurens Van Der Post (William Morrow and Co., 1958 and 1961). Some of the origin myths in Chapter Eleven are adaptations of those recorded by W. H. I. Bleek and L. C. Lloyd in *Specimens of Bushman Folklore* (London, George Allen and Company, Ltd., 1911).

Let me also thank Mr. and Mrs. L. K. Marshall for their hospitality and generosity in letting me see their vast reservoir of material on the Kung and for their patience in answering my questions.

My thanks to "Holly" Hollerorth, Curriculum Editor, Unitarian Universalist Association, under whose guidance this work was planned as part of a new curriculum. He has encouraged and assisted both me and the manuscripts through several years of effort.

And my thanks to my wife, Sue, for her unstinting help and for her many virtues, one of which is showing delight in the same things that delight me.

MAN THE CULTURE BUILDER PART II

A MULTIMEDIA CURRICULUM KIT   Ages 9–12

prepared by Walter L. Bateman

What is "culture"? How does one compare one culture with another? To what extent does a culture define the needs and shape the behavior of the people who live in it? *Man the Culture Builder, Part II*, is a multimedia curriculum designed to introduce children to some of the basic concepts of anthropology. It can show them the wonderful diversity of human life styles, and challenge them with questions about what it means to be human.

Part II is designed around the culture of the Kung Bushmen, a hunting-gathering people who roam the wastelands of the Kalahari desert in southern Africa. In learning how the Kung have adapted to life in their arid home, students will discover the vital part environment plays in a culture, and how that culture affects the way its people think and act.

Within the curriculum is a review of the basic ideas introduced through the Navajo culture, studied in *Part I.* By providing a framework for the comparison of cultures, *Man the Culture Builder* helps students understand that we, too, live in a culture, and that it affects our lives in much the same way that the Kung's and the Navajo's affects theirs.

Man the Culture Builder, Part II, consists of a teacher's manual and multimedia materials for a class of twenty, including a filmstrip, students' worksheets, and *The Kung of the Kalahari,* written especially as a part of this course.

For more information write to: Unitarian Universalist Association
25 Beacon Street, Boston, Massachusetts 02108